SYMBOLS

PLANT
CHARACTERS

The plant's
attraction is
its flowers

The plant's
attraction
is its fruits

Fragrant
rose

LIGHT
REQUIREMENTS

Sun

Shade

PLANT
CHARACTERS

Partial shade

Deciduous
shrub

Evergreen
shrub

MOISTURE
REQUIREMENTS

Semideciduous
shrub

Drought-
resistant

High moisture
requirements

Normal
moisture
requirements

ROSES

ROSES

Text by Václav Větvička

Illustrated by Petr Liška and Anna Skoumalová

ROSES
Original title Růže

Copyright © 1997 by Brio, spol. s r.o., Praha
© 1997 English edition Rebo Productions Ltd., London

Text by Václav Větvička
Illustrated by Petr Liška and Anna Skoumalová
Translated by Olga Kuthanová
Graphic layout and typesetting by Alfa
Colour separation by Repro plus, s.r.o.

ISBN 1 901094 54 5

Printed in Czech Republic.

CONTENTS

Foreword

Rose. Such a short word, and one that sounds practically the same in quite a number of languages! Rose, *ros, rós, roos, reuse, rhos, reus, rosa, roser, rozé, róža, rože, ruže...* all allegedly from the Greek word *rhodon* or perhaps also from the Sinhalese *rosa* or more likely the Aramaic *wardá*. I do not know, I'm not a linguist - and even linguists have never been able to agree on the matter. As for me, what I like is the old Greek legend according to which at one time there were only flowers with small blooms (something like violets), so-called ion, and ones with large blooms, so-called rhodon, roses and the rest.

If that was all there was to it, systematic botanists and schoolchildren would have an easy time. However, plant species number in the tens of thousands. The number of rose species alone is incalculable - this is due not to roses as such but to human imperfection. Whereas Carl von Linné, who established the system of classification of plants and animals, knew and named ten rose species, 150 years later the Frenchman Gandoger presumed there were as many as 5,000 species in Europe alone. It follows that man's view of nature varies and every classification into species and other systematic units will always be subjective and will no more than approximate the objective truth.

The only objective fact is that the rose is a woody plant occurring in roughly three different forms. The commonest are the so-called ramblers such as the dog rose (*Rosa canina*);

The leaves of wild and garden roses are odd-pinnate, usually with five or seven leaflets.

Roses without hooked thorns seek a place in the sun by forming spreading colonies.

when provided with a support they immediately make their way upward and grow, for example, to the top of a tree. In climbing they are aided by their hooked thorns and short flowering branches. Other roses form spreading colonies originating from a single seed and covering many square metres. And finally there are the roses of the third group that likewise originate from a single seed but branch beneath the soil surface, producing long underground runners from which a single rose about 50 cm high grows here and there above the surface.

They grow thus, without human aid, primarily in the northern hemisphere. Those growing south of the equator were introduced there by man. Man also began to cultivate roses, and to the original species, which objectively number only several dozen, added tens of thousands of cultivated garden varieties. It is these that are the subject of this book.

'Betty Uprichard' *(Dickson 1922) - a hybrid tea rose*

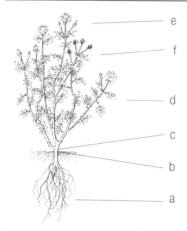

Parts of a cultivated rose bush: From the rootstock (a) grows the main stem (b) onto which the cultivated variety, or cultivar, was budded (c - bud union). Its shoots fork continuously up to the flower-bearing shoots (d). At the tips of these shoots either scant or rich flower clusters are formed (e) that later develop into hips (f).

The colour illustrations in the book faithfully depict actual specimens growing in the Rose nurseries of Václav Macháček in Prague.

No rose is without thorns

Characteristic of roses are the hard prickly protrusions on the stems called thorns. They are extraordinarily useful instruments for catching hold of something. They are not an adaptation serving as a protection from nibbling by animals, however, as was formerly believed. Roses whose strategy is based on climbing to the tops of trees developed thorns that are bent, crooked, or even hooked. Roses that form spreading colonies, on the other hand, developed thorns that are thin and straight but numerous, often supplemented with needle-like protrusions. Other roses, such as the wild Chinese rose *Rosa omeiensis*, were found to have relatively flat, wing-shaped thorns.

The variety *Rosa omeiensis* var. *pteracantha* (sometimes considered to be a cultivar, as it is not quite clear whether the fully outspread effect of the flat winged thorns has not been intentionally influenced by man) has highly ornamental thorns. Moreover they are translucent, wine-red, and on young branches extremely attractive viewed against the light.

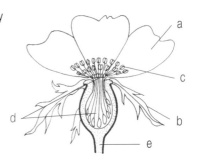

Longitudinal section of flower: a - petals, b - sepals, c - stamens, with anthers, d - pistils (ovaries, styles and stigmas), e - rudiments of the hip which is composed of the tissues of the plant stem, receptacle, and floral envelope.

Rose thorns: a - hooked (Rosa canina), b - straight (Rosa villosa), c - fine, prickly (Rosa pimpinellifolia), d - wing-shaped (Rosa omeiensis var. pteracantha).

Single bloom (left) and double bloom (right)

Structure of the flowers and hips

The flower of wild roses has an unusual structure. Already in the bud stage it contains the rudiments of a singular structure which develops into the ripened false fruit of the rose called the hip. This consists of a concave fleshy receptacle enclosing the pistils whose long styles grow out of the hip through its narrowed neck or "mouth". The calyx, which also participates in the formation of the hip, consists of five sepals, some of which are feather-like. From the top of the hip a large number of stamens and five petals grow, forming a single-flowered bloom.

Roses with double blooms have a greater number of petals usually at the cost of the stamens, i.e. some of the petals are modified stamens.

'Kordes Brillant'. *Kordes' shrub rose from 1983 with glowing, double blooms (35 petals) and delicate fragrance.*

Shapes of buds of cultivated roses: a - pointed, b - oblong to bottle-shaped, c - urceolate (urn-shaped), d - ovoid, e - globular.

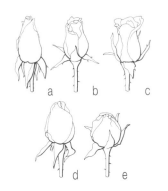

The number and size of the increased number of petals is also reflected in the structure of the bud of cultivated roses, one of the loveliest aspects of the rose. The shape of the bud is hereditary and typical of the given cultivar.

The characteristics of the bloom are of interest primarily to hybridisers and small growers. As a rule, spent blooms are removed and therefore do not develop into fruit. To those who wish to experiment with hybridising roses themselves or to pick the hips of wild roses growing in a hedgerow to brew a delicious tea, I should like to point out that the true fruits of the rose are not the hips, but the tiny stones (achenes is the precise botanical term) inside the hip.

Rootstock roses

From antiquity people have grown roses for pleasure. For nearly 2,000 years, however, gardeners were content to grow their ornamental roses either from seed (with the offspring bearing the characteristics of the parents) or they multiplied them by means of cuttings or division. The existing cultivated varieties sufficed for the purpose - and that their number was by no means small is borne out by the famed rose garden of Empress Josephine at Malmaison, her villa near Paris, which allegedly contained over 300 varieties or clones (nowadays they would be called cultivars), derived mostly from the Gallic or French rose (*Rosa gallica*).

Budding roses

A turning point in gardening, or rather only in rose growing technology, did not come about until lovely, warmth-loving roses were brought to

Flowering branch of a rootstock rose

Europe from the Far East, mainly from Southeast Asia. These roses were unable to withstand the harsher European climate and in the beginning there were too few of them to make division or the taking of cuttings possible. Gardeners therefore seized upon the method used with success at that time in fruit- growing - namely budding. Consider the advantage: whereas for division one needs at least one main stem with its readily separated root system and for cuttings a section of stem with several buds, in budding each bud taken from the parent plant will ultimately grow into an individual with characteristics identical to those of the parent plant. There is, of course, one more condition to fulfil: suitable rootstock should be available. This must be a plant that will not reject the foreign tissue, will unite with it and will nourish it so well that it develops into a new individual.

Rosa rugosa 'Hollandica'

Rootstocks

Despite their great variety in shape, roses are biochemically, or metabolically, very homogenous, and so it turned out that every rose is suitable rootstock for every other rose. The only thing that matters is that the rose to be used as rootstock has a good root system and is itself sufficiently resistant to diseases, pests, and climate - apart from that, it is quite possible to use any rose for this purpose, with the exception of, perhaps, standard roses where the rootstock must have at least some slight trunk-forming properties.

It was then up to the gardeners to make their work more agreeable by seeking out or selecting such types of roses as had few thorns or almost none, as these hindered the budders' work. If provided with sufficient prepared material (cultivated varieties and prepared rootstock), an experienced budder is capable of budding as many as several hundred roses in a single working day.

Today's modern cultivars of garden roses are in most instances already so hardy that they can also be grown on their own roots, generally from cuttings. For economic reasons, however, budding will probably be the only suitable, albeit laborious, method of making the most from a limited supply of raw material for many years to come.

The European dog rose (*Rosa canina*) was found to be suitable as rootstock for European conditions. Not till later were others added to the list, e.g. *Rosa multiflora*. Most fulfilled the conditions of hardiness, resistance to the harsher climate, having a good root system, and not being prone to disease, and they retained the uniformity of the seed even when sown broadcast.

Rosa canina

'Brögs Stachellose'

This rootstock rose was developed as early as 1902 by the R. Brög company of Reckenbach, Germany. It differs from the wild species (*Rosa canina*) mainly in being practically thornless. This is welcomed by budders, who do not injure their hands when handling such rootstock. Its flowers are single, nearly pure white, tinged with pink only in the bud, with deeply notched petals. The hips are classic, narrowly ovoid and dark red; they ripen early, becoming soft, and contain an average of about 20 achenes.

This rose has proved to be good rootstock for greenhouse cultivation, where it is possible to make good use of its long growing period. Outdoors it is somewhat less resistant to low temperatures.

Rosa canina
'Brögs Stachellose'

Rosa canina
'Inermis'

Rosa canina

'Inermis'

One of the European rootstock roses that have stood the test of time. It was first cultivated by the French firm of Gamon of Lyon in about 1905. The characteristics of this rose correspond to those of the wild species, but with a minimum number of thorns; some individuals are even completely thornless. The foliage is healthy, the root system substantial, the flowers single, pale pink. The hips are red, narrowly ellipsoid; they ripen late and contain about 20 achenes.

Rosa canina 'Inermis' is a good rootstock rose for practically all cultivars and is especially suitable for climbing roses. It has a long growing period and is occasionally susceptible to rust. It is not suitable for dry soils.

150 - 250 cm

***R**osa canina* **'Pollmers' is perhaps the commonest rootstock rose in Central Europe. It is also known by the name *Rosa pollmeriana*, after the Pollmer company of Grossenhain, Germany, but this name is invalid.**

Rosa canina

'Pollmers'

This again is a rose with all the characteristics of the wild species *Rosa canina*. Seedlings grown from seed sown broadcast are absolutely identical and suitable for large-scale nursery production. Unlike the preceding rootstocks, it is slightly thorny, the thorns are somewhat curved to hooked. The flowers are white and slightly larger than in the wild species, with a shallow notch on the margin of each petal. In rainy weather the centres of the flowers

are tinged reddish to carmine, this being a typical identifying feature of this rose. The hips are red, ovoid, fairly large, and contain 25 or more achenes.

In general this is a very vigorous, hardy rootstock rose with a substantial root system, somewhat more prone to fungal disease, especially black spot and rust.

Rosa coriifolia

'Froebelii'

This rose is still presented here under the above name although according to the current classification of European roses the correct name is *Rosa dumalis* subsp. *coriifolia* 'Froebelii'. While on the subject of nomenclature, it should also be pointed out that this rose was for a long time known by the incorrect names *Rosa laxa* hort. or *Rosa dumetorum* 'Laxa'.

It is a time-tested rootstock rose. It began to be used and later also sold by the Froebel company of Zurich as long ago as 1890! It was probably found in the wild amidst a population of local dog roses. It has few thorns and may even be thornless;

Rosa coriifolia 'Froebelii'

Rosa canina 'Pollmers',
colour of the flowers in
rainy weather

Rosa canina 'Pollmers',
ripening hips

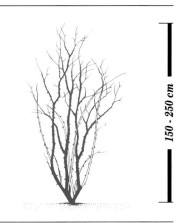

the foliage is greyish to mat green, the leaves are hairy on the underside along the midrib. The flowers are white or pale pink, rather small, and arranged in clusters of several blooms. The hips are ellipsoid to oblong-ovoid with about 25 achenes. The drying, slightly erect sepals remain on the tips of the hips until late in the autumn. This is suitable rootstock for growing roses, particularly on lime-rich soil. The colour of the blooms of hybrid teas grown on this rootstock is said to be exceptionally lovely.

150 - 250 cm

***R**osa multiflora* is the ancestor of multiflowered bedding roses and in some countries (e.g. Sweden) also a popular rootstock. *Rosa rubiginosa*, on the other hand, is an interesting rather than a common rootstock rose.

Rosa rubiginosa

Rosa rubiginosa is generally very thorny, particularly at the base of the stems. The large hooked thorns are interspersed with small, needle-like thorns. Its one great advantage, however, is that it has a deep root system that is very tolerant of limy soil. It is native to Europe, where it grows wild chiefly in limy localities. It has lovely dark pink to wine-red flowers arranged in scant clusters. The flower stalks as well as hips are usually covered with stalked glands. Also glandular are the very typical orbicular leaves. All the glands give off a strong apple-like scent from the time the leaves emerge until the last leaf dries up. The dry, erect sepals remain on the hips, which contain some 20 achenes, long after the first frost. This rose used to be recommended as rootstock particularly for large-flowered bedding roses; it was already in use as rootstock before 1675!

Rosa multiflora

Rosa multiflora is native to the Far East, China and Japan among others. It was used as rootstock by the Willmott company in England as early as 1875. It is a vigorous shrub, or rather rambler, which, unless it is provided with a support, has long arching annual shoots. The leaves, composed of seven to nine leaflets, have typical stipules with pectinately fringed margins. This is a dominant hereditary characteristic and it has been retained by many Polyantha cultivars. The flowers are small, white, and arranged in clusters of 30 or even more.

The hips are small, the size of a pea, and contain only a few achenes.

Hips of Rosa rubiginosa

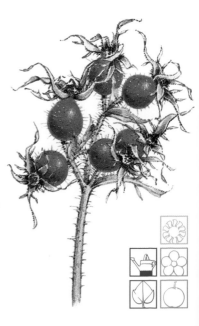

Rosa multiflora

Hips of Rosa multiflora

Rosa multiflora was a rootstock popular with nurserymen for roses which bore its genetic traits, in other words for Polyanthas and other multiflowered bedding roses and for climbers. Its thorniness, which was not particularly pronounced, was not too bothersome for the workers; for that matter, thornless lines are also cultivated. Cultivars budded onto this rose are of vigorous growth but the blooms are usually not well coloured. Rosa multiflora itself is susceptible to certain fungal diseases.

150 - 250 cm

Shrub roses

The category of shrub roses is very heterogeneous, embracing every rose that is neither a bedding rose (large-flowered or multiflowered), climber, or dwarf. The one trait they have in common is that they are highly resistant to disease as well as to low temperatures and they can be grown as large shrubs, generally 150-200 cm high, suitable for planting both in groups and as solitary specimens in large gardens and parks.

In habit they are quite like the shrubs of many original wild species and not without cause, because most of them are derived directly from those species. Lastly, many wild species or intraspecific taxons, i.e. subspecies, varieties, and forms, meet all the strictest aesthetic criteria and can be planted in the garden directly from the wild. One example that speaks for all is *Rosa rugosa*.

Hybrids

Other wild roses are crossed with certain cultivated varieties of bedding roses (large-flowered as well as multiflowered) and are named and classed according to the specific name of the wild species used, e.g. Rugosa-hybrids (as well as Hybrid Rugosa - in the US), Pimpinellifolia-hybrids, and the like. In gardening catalogues they are designated also by the letter S, derived either from the English word shrubs or the German word Strauchrosen.

Old roses

The so-called old roses undoubtedly belong to the category of shrub roses. Roses were popular and widely grown in Europe even before imports from the Far East started. Heading the list were roses derived from the Gallic or French rose, *Rosa gallica*, e.g. *Rosa* x *alba* and *Rosa* x *centifolia*, that are grown in Europe to this day. For many centuries they were practically the only cultivated roses.

Flowering branch of an old rose

Rosa x *centifolia, one of the very old cultivars that cannot be identified more precisely.*

They were grown for both ornamental (e.g. the so-called *Rosa mundi, Rosa gallica* 'Versicolor' with red and white striped flowers) and medicinal purposes (*Rosa gallica* var. *officinalis*, called the apothecary's rose or the rose of Provins or Provence).

Another famous old rose is the damask rose (*Rosa* x *damascena*), grown traditionally in Bulgaria for the production of attar of roses from its flowers.

Like these roses, the old double cultivar *Rosa majalis* 'Foecundissima', sometimes called the empire rose, is grown to this day, at least in the foothills of the Alps and in rural districts of neighbouring regions. Equally popular are the yellow Persian roses (*Rosa foetida*), whose double cultivar 'Persian Yellow' is perhaps the oldest cultivated ornamental plant of all - and yet it meets the criteria of modern shrub roses.

Rosa x *alba* and *Rosa* x *centifolia* are very old roses, known, perhaps, already in antiquity. They are among the first ten roses described by Carl von Linné himself and not one was absent from rural gardens from the Vosges to the Carpathians and from the Baltic regions to the Mediterranean.

Rosa x *alba*

The roots of this rose are to be found somewhere in the Caucasus region. *Rosa* x *alba* is a shrub about 150-200 cm high with upright stems and mat green leaves with five, occasionally seven leaflets. The small flowers in multiflowered clusters are double, the petals white and faintly scented. The flower stalks are longly glandular and thorny. The hips, if they are not completely sterile, contain only few achenes. This rose is fully frost-resistant, is not susceptible to any diseases, and has no special soil requirements.

Rosa x *centifolia*

In Europe *Rosa* x *centifolia* was for centuries one of the few sources of cultivated, ornamental roses. Its origin and past are veiled in mystery: its origins may lie in the Caucasus region or in Asia Minor, or perhaps in southern Europe... the possibilities are many. Most botanists are of the opinion that it is a double mutation of *Rosa gallica*. In view of the fact that the centifolia has been grown in gardens for so many centuries it is hardly surprising that the small number of surviving centifolias differ from the gallica in many respects. Perhaps the largest collection in history was the one Empress Josephine had at Malmaison at the close of the 18th century.

According to some reports it contained over 300 cultivars. Nowadays these truly historic roses are once again the object of interest on the part of collectors and amateur rose growers, who are to be found mainly in Germany, focused around Hedi and Wernt Grimm and the VDR (Verein Deutscher Rosenfreunde, the Association of German Friends of the Rose).

Rosa x *centifolia* formed thinly

Rosa x *centifolia*

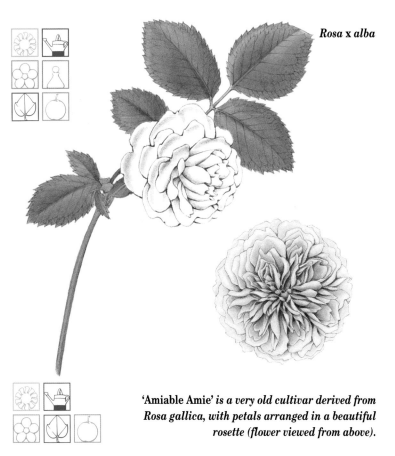

Rosa x *alba*

'Amiable Amie' *is a very old cultivar derived from*
Rosa gallica, with petals arranged in a beautiful
rosette (flower viewed from above).

branched, not very tall shrubs with stiff
papery leaves generally composed of
five leaflets. The flowers, the basic
colour of which was pink, were double,
though they never numbered a hundred
as suggested by their name: the
greatest number I have ever been able
to ascertain was 60-odd petals in one
bloom. These roses, however, are
extremely hardy, vital, practically
untouched by disease. To this day they
are often found growing in places where
they are the sole witness to a one-time
settlement.

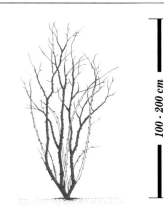

100 - 200 cm

A significant role in the history of the cultivation of shrub roses was played by the German firm of W. Kordes, which consistently devoted itself to the breeding of frost-resistant shrub roses and was famous chiefly for those derived from the wild rose *Rosa pimpinellifolia* var. *altaica*. Crossing this with large-flowered hybrid teas (such as 'Joanna Hill') produced a whole group of "spring" shrub roses, for example 'Frühlingsduft', 'Frühlingsmorgen', and others.

'Frühlingsmorgen'

Another of the Kordes shrub roses, dating back to 1941. As mentioned above, what is characteristic of the whole group is the use of the wild Siberian rose *Rosa pimpinellifolia* var. *altaica*. In this case the wild rose was pollinated with the pollen of an unnamed seedling (characteristics unknown), derived from crossing the red hybrid tea 'E.G. Hill' and the deep scarlet hybrid tea 'Cathrine Kordes'. The new rose has the classic single

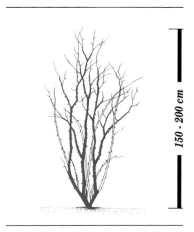

150 - 200 cm

'Frühlingsmorgen'

'Frühlingsgold'

flowers typical of the wild species,
pinkish-carmine with whitish-yellow
centre and brownish-red anthers,
strikingly large, up to 11 cm across,
and not very fragrant. The leaves are
mat greyish green, the habit shrub-like,
up to 180 cm high.

Though it flowers only once
a year, this is an excellent rose for
planting as a solitary specimen or in
groups on slopes.

'Frühlingsgold'

The oldest Kordes shrub rose is
derived from the wild Siberian *Rosa
pimpinellifolia* var. *altaica*. It has been

cultivated since 1937. The female
parent, *Rosa pimpinellifolia* var. *altaica*,
itself creamy white, was pollinated with
the pollen of the yellow hybrid tea
'Joanna Hill'. The rose produced by
this crossing has single to faintly semi-
double, open, saucer-shaped blooms
up to 10 cm across and coloured
golden yellow. It flowers very early and
produces a profusion of blooms, but
only once a year. The dense, slightly
spreading, upright shrub attains
a height of 3 m; the leaves are small
and mat green.

The development of 20th-century shrub roses was the work of a large number of hybridisers, who met with varied success. Practically every one of them, however, started out with some wild species of desirable habit, vigour and hardiness to which qualities they tried to add the basic characteristic of cultivated roses, namely large double blooms. The cultivars 'Erfurt' and 'Nevada' are two successful examples.

'Nevada'

The white-flowering shrub rose' 'Nevada' is a product of the 20th century, one that is so successful that it is to be found in practically every park from San Francisco to Paris or Moscow.

This by now historic rose has interesting origins: P. Dot, a Spanish breeder in Barcelona, pollinated his own hybrid tea, the pink cultivar 'La Giralda', with the pollen of the East Asian *Rosa moyesii* and named the new cultivar

'Nevada'. This was sometime before 1927. Certain sources claim, however, that the species used for the crossing was not the wild *Rosa moyesii* but its tetraploid mutant 'Farggesii'. The hybrid - 'Nevada' - has small ovoid buds coloured pink or apricot; in full bloom the flowers are practically pure white. Sometimes, however, they are flushed a delicate pink on the reverse. They are strikingly large (up to 13 cm across), slightly semi-double, opened outward, unscented. They grow singly or in scant clusters, but they are always produced

'Nevada'

'Erfurt'

in great profusion. Some years flowering is repeated again in late summer, but it is not as abundant. The shrub grows to a height of 250 cm, some of the stems are arching. The foliage is abundant, ornamental, pale mat green.

'Erfurt'

The shrub rose 'Erfurt' was considered to be a rose of the *Rosa moschata* group. *Rosa moschata* was frequently used as one of the parents of garden roses even though its true origin is uncertain - perhaps it was Asia Minor or the Near East. The cultivar 'Erfurt' was developed by the Kordes company in Germany in 1939 by pollinating the female parent - the cultivar 'Eva' - with the pollen of the climbing hybrid tea cultivar 'Réveil Dijonnais'. The new shrub rose had strikingly long pointed buds, large semi-double flowers with pink petals, yellowish at the base, opened flat, arranged in many-flowered clusters, and with a strong musky fragrance. The shrub is of spreading habit with 150 to 200-cm-long stems, stiff, leathery green leaves, young leaves tinted bronze to purple.

150 - 250 cm

Hybrid tea and other large-flowered bedding roses

The history of the group of garden roses called hybrid teas begins in the Far East, in China, India, Southeast Asia. It is generally believed that the ancestors of the large-flowered garden roses were the wild species *Rosa chinensis* and *Rosa odorata*. Whereas the former probably still exists and grows wild to this day, the latter is something of a mystery. In the literature and in herbals roses are shown of such different qualities, that even I and my much more qualified predecessors have been unable to decide in this "paternity suit".

The above-mentioned *Rosa odorata* can also be found under the names of *Rosa gigantea* (reputedly it may attain a height of up to 15 m!) or *Rosa indica* (the entire section of these evergreen subtropical roses takes its name, Indicae, from this rose). Some botanists believe that *Rosa gigantea* was at one time crossed, perhaps in Burma, India, or China, with *Rosa chinensis,* giving rise to *Rosa x odorata*. As *Rosa gigantea* is considered at times to be merely a synonym of *Rosa odorata*, and at other times an independent species, one might conclude that *Rosa x odorata* is simultaneously both its own mother and daughter. I therefore suggest that we admit defeat and conclude that the Adam and Eve of large-flowered (and

Bud and fully opened bloom of a hybrid tea rose

**'Las Vegas' *(Kordes 1981)*,
large-flowered hybrid tea rose,
registered trademark**

**'Nocturno' *(Swim 1947)*,
large-flowered hybrid tea rose**

perhaps also other) garden roses are unknown.

The Italian botanist Savi of Florence gave these roses (*Rosa* x *odorata*) another name - *Rosa thea*. Why they reminded him of a tea plant (*Thea sinensis*) I have been unable to discover so far and I have no other explanation for his giving this name to the species. It was decidedly not because of the colour of the flowers, which was pink. The name he selected could not be recognised by botany because it was put forward at a time when these roses were already known by other names. However, these roses continued to be known as 'tea' roses. That name survived all long-forgotten cultivars; there even came a time when it was applied only to roses with "tea-coloured" blooms, but that was later, long after Savi proposed the name.

In the United States, and under its influence also elsewhere, large-flowered garden roses fulfilling the criteria of hybrid teas are classed in the group called *Grandiflora* - but that is what this chapter is all about:

"Large-flowered bedding roses have well-formed buds, flowers usually borne singly or as many as three to a stem, and are generally used for cutting" - that is a simple definition that fits even today's European hybrid teas. In catalogues they are designated Th or TH (in Europe) or HT (in the US, where large-flowered bedding roses are furthermore designated Gr).

White large-flowered bedding roses

"Hybrid tea" is purely a gardeners' term for what is known as the Queen of Flowers. This designation coupled with the name rose can belong to none other: dog roses and wild roses as such are too unpretentious for a royal title and perhaps nondescript as well, and other groups of roses, no matter how highly bred, are no match when it comes to size and fragrance of the blooms.

'Virgo'

The cultivar 'Virgo' is a typical hybrid tea of the mid-20th century. It was developed by the French firm of Mallerin and put on the market in 1947. Two years later it won its first gold medal. Its parents were the white cultivars 'Blanche Mallerin' and 'Neige Parfum'. In some catalogues it is listed also under the name of 'Virgo Liberationem'. It is a moderately vigorous rose with weak thorns reaching a height of about 70 cm. The leaves are semi- glossy dark green, the bud on a thick stalk is slender, conical, up to 5 cm long, often tinted pink. In full bloom the flower is large, up to 12 cm across, semi-double, composed of 24-30 pure white petals.

It has a very delicate fragrance and cut flowers last about five days. This rose is less resistant to low temperatures and black spot, but highly resistant to mildew. It is grown as a bedding rose, in collections, and for cutting. The derived climbing cultivar 'Climbing Virgo' was put on the market in 1957.

'Pascali'

The white cultivar 'Pascali' was developed by L. Lens of Belgium in 1963. The cultivar is the product of crossing the pink cultivar 'Queen Elizabeth' with the white 'White Butterfly'. It is a vigorous bush about 70 cm high with semi-glossy dark green foliage. The buds are oblong, pointed, beautifully shaped, up to 6 cm long, the flowers are double, opened out flat, and

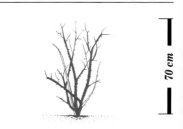

70 cm

'Virgo'

'Pascali'

composed of 30 or more creamy-white petals. The flowers are sometimes borne singly, more often, however, in clusters of a few to as many as seven blooms. This is a moderately hardy rose good mainly for growing in beds.

Garden "tea roses" were cultivated chiefly in the first half of the 19th century. Founder of this group was the white variety 'Devoniensis' of 1838. Of course, at the time other groups of garden roses were also cultivated, derived, as a rule, from *Rosa chinensis* (introduced to Europe as early as 1759). They were called Noisettes, Bourbons, Remontants, amongst others, and they rivalled tea roses. It was the crossing of the remontant 'Mme Victor Verdier' with the tea rose 'Mme Bravy' that in 1867 produced the silvery-pink variety 'La France', considered to be the founder of the entire contemporary group of large-flowered garden roses called hybrid teas ever since.

'John F. Kennedy'

In 1965, not long after the tragic death of J.F. Kennedy, the Oregon firm of Jackson and Perkins put on the market a white cultivar developed by the American breeder Boemer and named in honour of the assassinated president. One of the parents was an unnamed seedling, the other the white cultivar 'White Queen'.

'John F. Kennedy' is a vigorous, healthy rose up to 80 cm high with fairly narrow, leathery, dark green leaves.

'John F. Kennedy'

'Mount Shasta'

The ovoid buds are a cool white, often with a greenish tinge, the flowers measure up to 12 cm, are prominently double, composed of 45 to 50 pure white, moderately fragrant petals. The cultivar is patented in the US under the number 2441.

'Mount Shasta'

It is amazing the names some roses are given. That they are named after a popular president or close woman friend is quite understandable.

80 cm

Nevertheless nearly ten cultivated roses bear the names of mountains: apart from 'Mount Shasta' we have 'Mount Everest' and 'Mount St. Helena'.

The white cultivar 'Mount Shasta' is a typical American large-flowered bedding rose. It was put on the market by the Swim and Weeks company of California in 1963 and was immediately patented under number 2132. In a way it is closely related to the cultivars 'Virgo' and 'Pascali', for it shares at least one parent with each: one is the pink 'Queen Elizabeth', the other the white 'Blanche Mallerin'. This is a very hardy, upright rose with greyish-green, leathery leaves. The buds are long-pointed, the flowers large, semi-double, composed of 20 to 26 fragrant pure white petals.

Yellow large-flowered bedding roses

Even though yellow roses are not a rare sight in the wild, the colour yellow in cultivated roses was for a long time an unattainable dream. It was the Frenchman Pernet-Ducher who in the 1890s produced the first yellow large-flowered bedding rose.

'King's Ransom'

'King's Ransom'

This yellow rose was produced in Santa Rosa, California, and put on the market in 1961. It was developed by crossing the golden-yellow cultivar 'Golden Masterpiece' and the saffron-yellow cultivar 'Lydia'. 'King's Ransom' is a vigorous rose up to 90 cm high with large, glossy, light green leaves. The buds are oblong-ovoid, up to 5 cm long, the flowers glowing golden-yellow, glossy, strikingly large (sometimes up to 15 cm), double (35-40 petals) borne singly or in clusters of as many as five, and with a strong fragrance. This cultivar is patented under American patent number 2103 and in 1962 was one of the top American roses (AARS, All-American Rose Selection). It is good for bedding as well as cutting.

'Oregold'

One of the loveliest yellow hybrid teas to date was produced by Mathias Tantau in Germany before 1975 and soon after this rose won out in competition with top American roses. Its parents were bicoloured roses - the red-yellow 'Piccadilly' and the coral-orange with cream reverse 'Königin der

'Oregold'

'Landora'

Rosen' whose "blood-line"
includes, among others, the famous
'Super Star'. 'Oregold' has pointed
ovoid buds, warm golden-yellow
flowers on long stalks, a pleasant
fragrance, and quality foliage. In
following years it was tested throughout
practically the whole of the US with the
verdict that it is a moderately to
extraordinarily hardy rose, but that its
flowers open rapidly and are soon spent
in warmer situations or hot weather. All
the testers, however, agreed that the
yellow colour of this rose is matchless.

'Landora'

It is not simply by chance that this
selection includes two yellow roses
produced by M. Tantau. It testifies to
the concentrated, tenacious work of the
well-known Holstein firm. 'Landora' was

put on the market in 1970 as the
product of an unnamed seedling
(unfortunately of unknown
characteristics) and the above-
mentioned yellow hybrid tea 'King's
Ransom'. It is a rose of a somewhat
cooler, but constant, non-fading yellow
hue, with large, strikingly double flowers
(35-50 petals) produced without fail.
The buds are conical, the blooms grow
singly or in scant clusters. This is
a vigorous rose of moderate height
(60 cm), greatly branched, with foliage
a light green flushed with bronze; it is
definitely frost resistant and fairly
resistant to mildew and black spot. It is
used as a bedding rose in large group
plantings.

Pink large-flowered bedding roses

Breeding roses requires not only extensive knowledge but also imagination, talent for combining, and above all a fortunate choice of seedlings.

'Lancôme'

This magnificent hybrid tea with well-formed bud on a long, sturdy stalk, is an important rose of the past decade. It was put on the market in 1986, even though its "birth certificate" mentions a quite different date: according to some sources it first saw the light of day in the garden of the well-known Parisian breeder Delbard-Chabert as long ago as 1973. It is the result of many years of selective breeding in which probably the female parent, the pink-red cultivar 'Dr Albert Schweitzer', played the main role. The male parent was some unnamed seedling, the offspring of two other unknown seedlings and a rose designated as MEIneed x 'Present Filial'. 'Lancôme' is a healthy, upright, moderately double (28 petals),

80 - 100 cm

practically unscented, dark red rose, good primarily for cultivation and forcing in the greenhouse.

'Jacaranda'

Kordes' delicately violet-pink 'Jacaranda' (sometimes listed also as 'Jacakor') has been cultivated since 1985. Its parents were two unnamed seedlings. Typical of 'Jacaranda' is the classic form of the flower, which is large, double (35 petals) and fragrant. The habit of the cultivar is upright, its foliage medium green.

'Queen Elizabeth'

"Bessy" is one of the best-known roses of all, often more regally called The Queen Elizabeth Rose. It was developed by Dr W.E. Lammerts at Livermore, California, before 1954, when it was put on the market. In 1955 it was already selected as one of the top American roses of the year and won gold medals at exhibitions in 1956, 1957, 1960, 1968, amongst others. It was developed by crossing the red hybrid tea 'Charlotte Armstrong' with the vermilion floribunda 'Floradora'. It is

'Lancôme'

'Jacaranda'

'Queen Elizabeth'

a typical American large-flowered bedding rose of upright habit (up to 100 cm high) with glossy dark green, leathery foliage. The buds are pointed, the flowers double (as many as 40 petals), carmine-pink to salmon-pink, 8-10 cm across, the colour fading with age. They are rarely borne singly, generally several to a stem on slender stalks.

This cultivar is resistant to variable weather as well as fungal disease. It is grown as a bedding rose and for cutting; its uncommon size makes it a good rose also for small solitary groups.

Red large-flowered bedding roses

Located at Cap d'Antibes in France's Maritime Alps are the famed Meilland nurseries where many roses were developed, each with the typical French charm.

'Christian Dior'

'Christian Dior'

One of Meilland's famous roses is the red cultivar 'Christian Dior', put on the market already in 1958. It is the "child" of three parents. A. Meilland crossed his 'Rouge Meilland' with 'Kordes Sondermeldung', and then 'Rouge Meilland' with 'Gloria Dei' (also a Meilland rose). Then he crossed the offspring of the two aforesaid crossings and the result was 'Christian Dior'. Not the famed couturier but a magnificent red rose, awarded the gold medal in Geneva the year it came out. It is a vigorous, moderately hardy rose about 70 cm high with dark green leaves and characteristic conical buds on long sturdy stalks.

The flower is double (over 40 petals), deep red to velvety red,

70 - 80 cm

'Papa Meilland'

'Black Lady'

faintly scented, and opens slowly. It is a good garden rose and suitable for cutting, but only when the flowers start to bloom, otherwise it tends to wilt.

flowers large, double (more than 35 petals) and with a strong fragrance. This is a vigorous rose (80 cm) with firm, leathery, glossy olive-green leaves.

'Papa Meilland'

With this beautiful rose Alan Meilland paid more than sufficient tribute to the "old man". Put on the market in 1963, it was the product of crossing the superb dark red California rose 'Chrysler Imperial' and another deep red rose - 'Charles Mallerin', likewise from the Meilland nurseries. The outcome could be none other than one of the famous deep velvety red roses. The buds are pointed and the

'Black Lady'

One of the extremely lovely deep to black-red roses of the second half of the 20th century was developed by the German breeder Tantau - it was put on the market in 1976 and was patented; its parentage is apparently a production secret. The buds are plump to globular, the flowers moderately large, double, blackish velvety red, and extremely fragrant. The habit is bushy, the foliage mat green.

Glowing red large-flowered bedding roses

The flowers of most classic large-flowered roses were and continue to be soft to pastel hues. Roses of glowing colours, mostly vermilion-red, represented a breakthrough in this realm of subdued tones.

'Super Star'

Since 1960 perhaps no rose nursery and probably no publication on roses got by without this, one of the most famous roses of all time. Perhaps it could not have any name other than 'Super Star'; the synonym 'Tropicana' has practically fallen into oblivion. 'Super Star' was developed in the Tantau nurseries of Holstein, Germany. It is the product of the complicated crossing of two bastards, unnamed seedlings of unknown characteristics, and two famous roses: the most famous of all - the yellow-pink 'Gloria Dei' and the vermilion 'Alpenglühen'

from which it probably inherited its colour.

It forms an upright bush about 70 cm high with mat dark green foliage. The buds are slender conical, up to 7 cm long, the flowers up to 12 cm across, double, composed of an average of 42 petals coloured glowing salmon-red.

The blooms have a pleasant fragrance and are resistant to the effects of the weather; cut blooms last about a week. The rose's resistance to frost, mildew, and black spot is practically 100 per cent. The number of gold medals and awards won by this rose runs into the dozens (in 1960 alone it won perhaps all important competitions). In the US it is patented under number 1969.

'Duke of Windsor'

Though 'Duke of Windsor' is a purely English title, the rose that goes

'Super Star'

'Duke of Windsor'

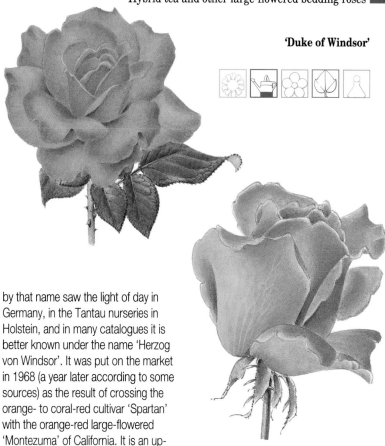

'Alexander'

by that name saw the light of day in Germany, in the Tantau nurseries in Holstein, and in many catalogues it is better known under the name 'Herzog von Windsor'. It was put on the market in 1968 (a year later according to some sources) as the result of crossing the orange- to coral-red cultivar 'Spartan' with the orange-red large-flowered 'Montezuma' of California. It is an upright hybrid tea (80 cm) with pointed buds and not very double (28 petals) salmon-red blooms of classic form and pronounced fragrance. The foliage is glossy dark green and moderately disease-proof.

'Alexander'

When rose growers come up with a successful variety of a new interesting colour it becomes the subject of crossing, producing ever more hybrids and cultivars. That is also what the English firm of Harkness in Hitchin, Hertforshire, did: it crossed the then already famous 'Super Star' with the offspring of a cross between the semi-double pink 'Ann Elizabeth' and likewise semi-double yellow rose 'Allgold'. The result is a pale vermilion, faintly double (20 petals), moderately scented variety of upright habit with classic buds on long stalks and slightly glossy dark green foliage.

Silvery-blue large-flowered bedding roses

So far the attempts at growing a true "blue" rose have met only with partial success in the form of cultivars in various shades of silvery violet to dingy violet. Perhaps best known of the lot is 'Mainzer Fastnacht'. Some of these roses also have an interesting, quite different fragrance in that they smell of lemons.

'Mainzer Fastnacht'

This rose was developed by M. Tantau in Holstein, Germany, in 1964. The parentage of this cultivar is veiled in secrecy, for Tantau states he selected it from the offspring of a cross he performed between an unnamed seedling, offspring of the similar silvery cultivar 'Sterling Silver', and an unknown seedling.

That is rather an odd set of parents; perhaps, however, Mr. Tantau considers the parentage of this undoubtedly interesting cultivar his production secret. 'Mainzer Fastnacht' is a rose of spreading habit, only slightly over half a metre high. The leaves are leathery and faintly glossy light green. The ovoid buds are long-pointed, up to 6 cm long. The flowers are large, double (40 petals), coloured an unusual violet-blue with a silvery tinge, sometimes described as lilac. Appealing also is the fragrance of this rose, which has a faint lemony scent. It was awarded its first gold medal in Rome in 1964, the year it was introduced.

'Eminence'

This cultivar was introduced to the world in 1962 by R.R. Gaujard in Orléans, France. Amongst the silvery-

'Mainzer Fastnacht'

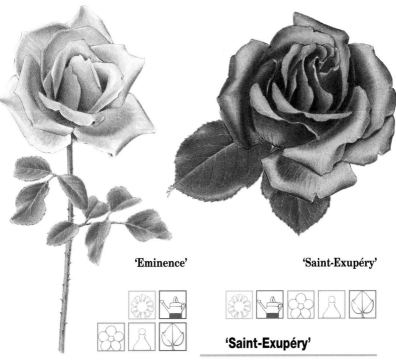

'Eminence'   'Saint-Exupéry'

'Saint-Exupéry'

violet hybrid teas it represents the extreme limit of that colour range, for it is usually described as lavender. To obtain this new variety, the breeder used one of his older cultivars - the pink 'Viola' - which he crossed with an unnamed seedling and then crossed their offspring with the world-famous, time-tested 'Gloria Dei'. In view of the blind spot of an unknown seedling in its parentage, one can only deduce that 'Eminence' inherits its unusual colour from that parent. It is a bush of upright habit with leathery, light green leaves and double (40 petals), pronouncedly scented flowers that are somewhat flat in full bloom.

A rose bearing this name could have been developed by none other than a French firm - Delbard-Chabert of Paris, in 1961. The complicated crossing involving two pairs (the pink 'Christopher Stone' x the saffron-yellow 'Marcelle Gret' and the pink single 'Holstein' x the salmon to apricot 'Bayadère') produced from each an unnamed seedling and the crossing of the two seedlings produced the unusually coloured cultivar 'Saint-Exupéry'. I think the breeder himself must have been surprised. It is truly a large-flowered rose (flowers up to 12 cm across), semi-double, with a delicate fragrance and hard-to-define colour generally described as silvery-lilac. It is of bushy habit.

Bronze-orange large-flowered bedding roses

Typical of the following three cultivars is not only the unusual colour of the blooms but also the glossy dark green foliage and extremely pleasant fragrance.

'Wiener Charme'

'Wiener Charme'

Located not far from Hamburg are the nurseries of Kordes and Sons, one of Germany's most important firms. That is where the hybrid tea 'Wiener Charme' was developed by crossing the orange-golden-yellow cultivar 'Chantré' with the golden-yellow 'Goldene Sonne'. It is a vigorously growing bush with reddish main stems 50 to 100 cm long. The buds are ovoid, the flowers borne singly or in clusters on sturdy stalks. The flowers themselves are very large (up to 15 cm across), not overly double (27 petals) and coloured coppery- or bronze-orange. The leaves are susceptible to black spot.

'Sutter's Gold'

'Sutter's Gold' certainly paid off for the California breeder Herbert C. Swim. Although it was put on the market nearly half a century ago (in 1950), it belongs to the basic repertoire of rose gardens as well as rose nurseries. It has won dozens of medals, mostly gold. It is the offspring of the cherry-red 'Charlotte Armstrong' and the apricot 'Signora'. The buds are of classic form, strikingly slender, up to 5.5 cm long, the flowers 8-14 cm across, composed of 30-35 golden-

70 - 90 cm

'Apricot Nectar'

'Sutter's Gold'

yellow petals with orange or bronze veining on the reverse, and with a strong fragrance. It is moderately vigorous, making rather loose main stems up to 80 cm long. It is more than moderately resistant to low temperatures and fungal diseases, and highly resistant to mildew. This is an excellent rose for cutting.

'Apricot Nectar'

The efforts of E.S. Boemer of the USA, were crowned with success when he developed a new rose round

1965, named 'Apricot Nectar' for the unusual apricot, bronze-tinted colour of its petals, by crossing an unnamed seedling with the very successful orange cultivar 'Spartan'. It has rather plump, ovoid buds that open into prominently double flowers (45 petals) about 10 cm across, with a pronounced fruity scent. It has a strong, broadly spreading bushy habit, with annual shoots up to 90 cm long. In the US, where it was selected as one of the best roses of the year already in 1966, it is patented under number 2594.

Bicoloured large-flowered bedding roses

The most famous and most successful rose of all time is 'Gloria Dei'. Over 100,000 were sold during the first 30 years of its existence and it continues to be widely grown to this day, even though it is more than fifty years old. Its history is equally well known: from the late 1930s systematic breeding was carried out at the Meilland nurseries at Cap d'Antibes in the south of France, the result of which was a rose initially named 'Mme A. Meilland'. It was the product of crossing an unnamed seedling with the cultivar 'Margaret McGredy'. The new rose did not catch on under the name 'Mme A. Meilland', perhaps because World War II was at its height. When it ended in 1945, the world breathed a sigh of relief as life returned to normal and Meilland captured the mood of the moment: he put the rose on the market under the name 'Gloria Dei' - Glory to God. That same year it was introduced also in the US, though under a different name but one with like connotation - 'Peace'.

'Gloria Dei'

This is a rose of spreading growth about 80-100 cm high with large glossy dark green leaves. The buds on long stout stems (the first flowers are borne on stems up to 50 cm long) are broadly conical. The flowers are large (even more than 15 cm), greatly double (over 50 petals), fragrant. The basic colour is golden yellow edged pink at first, later, towards autumn, the yellow fades and the pink colour spreads.

This rose won a gold medal under its old name (in 1944), and after 1945 there was not a single important world show at which it was not victorious. When the international federation of rose associations organised a contest of the best roses of all time in 1975, 'Gloria Dei' was the uncontested winner.

It is good for bedding, also grown as a solitary specimen, and on occasion also for cutting. It is highly resistant to cold, mildew, and black spot.

'Double Delight'

Even among bicoloured roses this cultivar is a curiosity, although admittedly an interesting one. It was

'Double Delight'

'Gloria Dei'

developed by Herbert C. Swim and introduced in 1977 by the Armstrong Nurseries of Ontario, California. That very same year this rose won the annual show of top American roses (AARS) in the US and at the shows in Rome and Baden-Baden it won a gold medal; in 1986 it won the James Alexander Gamble Rose Fragrance Award. Its parents were the cultivars 'Granada' and 'Garden Party'. The buds are long and pointed, the flowers large, double (30-45 petals), creamy-white giving way to strawberry pink,

with a spicy scent. The bush is of upright, robust habit, reaching a height of 100 cm.

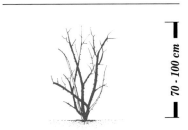

70 - 100 cm

The Northern Irish rose grower Sam McGredy apparently favoured bicoloured roses, the same as me; how otherwise can one explain his systematic work with the famed bicoloured rose 'Gloria Dei'? The results of his efforts are the two cultivars shown on these pages.

'Kronenbourg'

'Kronenbourg'

In 1965 McGredy found in his collection a spontaneous mutant of 'Gloria Dei' which he put on the market under the name 'Kronenbourg'. (In the US, where 'Gloria Dei' is known by the synonym 'Peace', the cultivar 'Kronenbourg' also goes by another name - in this case 'Flaming Peace', after its female parent.) It is a vigorous to robust rose 80 cm high with large, leathery, glossy green leaves. The buds are plump to ovoid, about 6 cm long, the flowers double, fragrant, bicoloured, (pale) yellow and purple to carmine- red. The distribution of the colours on the

petals of some blooms is much like that of the female parent cultivar (see 'Gloria Dei'), in other blooms the marginal petals are red with yellow reverse and the closer the petals are to the centre of the flower, the yellower they are - merely flushed with red.

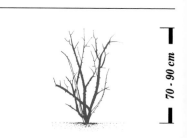

70 - 90 cm

'Piccadilly'

'Piccadilly'

In the late 1950s Sam McGredy crossed his yellow rose 'McGredy's Yellow' with the fragrant, deep scarlet cultivar 'Karl Herbst', offspring of the world's most famous rose 'Gloria Dei'. From the resulting offspring he selected the best and in 1960 put it on the market under the name 'Piccadilly'.

This is a low rose, about 40-50 cm high, of somewhat spreading habit with glossy deep green foliage.

The buds are pointed and about 5 cm long. The flowers are scarlet with golden-yellow red-veined reverse, double (25-30 petals), and are borne singly or as many as five to a stem; the stems are sturdy. The extraordinary beauty and colour combination won this rose several gold medals already the first year it was put on the market (1960) - in Madrid, Rome, and Great Britain. In gardens it is grown primarily as a bedding rose.

Multiflowered bedding roses

Gardeners are hard to figure out: on the one hand they tried to produce a rose with the largest possible flowers growing, inasmuch as possible, singly on long stems, and on the other hand they sought to obtain roses of low, compact habit that would form large heads of smaller but numerous flowers and would be suited to large beds.

These efforts were crowned with success, but not until after 1860: some believe it was already in that year, others are inclined to believe it was in 1865, and a third group is of the opinion it was not until 1868 or just before that the East Asian multiflowered rose *Rosa multiflora* was brought to Europe. That was the name given it by the well-known botanist Thunberg. (The specific name *multiflora* is derived from the Latin for multiflowered.) However, as so often happens in botany (and in gardening this is even more true) everyone wishes to gain some immortality by bestowing his or her name on a certain plant. Thus it happened that the botanists Siebold and Zuccarini each gave to the same plant basically the same name - *Rosa polyantha*, although they derived it from Greek. (Unfortunately for them, they were somewhat later.) In botany, though, names are governed by the so-called rule of priority: the name that is valid is the one that came first, and so this rose will remain known as *Rosa*

multiflora. To add to the language difficulties, suffice it to point out that *Rosa polyantha* is not the only synonym for this rose; in older literature it went by the names of *Rosa thunbergii, R. linkii, R. thyrsiflora, R. intermedia, R. wichuriae, R. microcarpa, R. dawsoniana, R. franchetii paniculigera*, etc.

Flowering branch of a multiflowered bedding rose

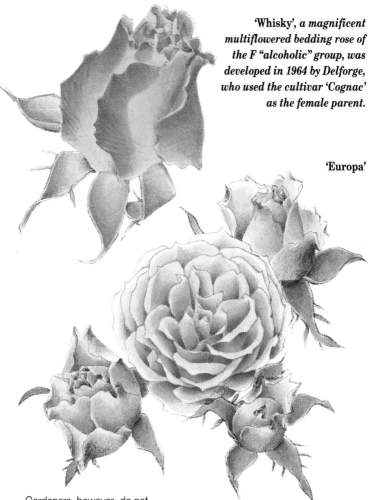

'Whisky', *a magnificent multiflowered bedding rose of the F "alcoholic" group, was developed in 1964 by Delforge, who used the cultivar 'Cognac' as the female parent.*

'Europa'

Gardeners, however, do not observe the rules of botany too strictly and to this day grow and breed what were first called Polyanthas and currently also the more complex hybrid Polyanthas. Because the differences between the individual classes long ago became blurred and indistinct, probably the most suitable name for this class is the name currently used officially, i.e. multiflowered bedding roses. They are roses that have several or many flowers to a single stem and are grown in the garden in beds and in parks in large expanses - however only few are good for cutting. In catalogues they are generally designated by the letters P or Pol. (Polyanthas), PH (Polyantha hybrids) or F (floribundas - roses ranging between multiflowered and large-flowered bedding roses).

White multiflowered bedding roses

Multiflowered bedding roses proved a veritable treasure for breeders by virtue of their singular traits: the rose had long, slender annual shoots, was more resistant to lower temperatures than the large-flowered bedding roses of more southern climes, and above all the blooms were in clusters of sometimes as many as several dozen flowers. No matter that they were small; this was a characteristic that could be corrected by suitable hybridisation. Compared with the south Asian and European roses, which have at most ten to twelve flowers to a stem, this was something!

'Schneewittchen'

The Polyantha 'Schneewittchen' is probably one of the oldest roses of this class: it is amazing that after nearly a century it is still so popular. It was developed by the German firm of P. Lambert in Trier. The parents were the currently century-old (1896), yellowish 'Aglaia', a direct descendent

'Schneewittchen'

'Dagmar Späth'

of *Rosa multiflora*, and a seedling that was the product of a prior crossing of the two cultivars 'Paquerette' and 'Souvenir de Mme Levet'. The resulting rose was distinctly multiflowered, double, white both in the bud and in full bloom, gradually becoming flushed with yellow and turning pale yellow with age. The flowers open out flat and are very plentiful.

'Dagmar Späth'

At the nurseries of the firm of Wirtz and Eicke at Rödenheim near Frankfurt, the time-tested pink cultivar 'Joseph Guy' unexpectedly produced a mutant, a white-flowered sport that was named 'Dagmar Späth'. This is a pure white multiflowered bedding rose at one time classed in the floribunda category with short, rather ovoid buds

and double flowers that are pure white at first, flushed pink with age; the petals are wavy on the margin. There are a great many flowers to each cluster. This is a 45 to 50-cm-high, spreading bush with shoots and leaves reddish at first, later green and hardy. It is a good rose for large beds.

50 cm

Yellow multiflowered bedding roses

The first low bedding Polyantha was probably the variety 'Paquerette' which saw the light of day in 1875. It is said that it was a cross between *Rosa multiflora* and *Rosa chinensis* var. *minima*. The reverse crossing (male and female switched roles) is said to have given rise to another historic Polyantha, the variety 'Mignonette' - and that is the founder of all present Polyanthas, Polyantha hybrids (developed in the years 1910-1925 by crossing the original tea roses with Polyanthas), as well as floribundas (these were developed by crossing Polyantha hybrids with hybrid teas and made their appearance on the world scene after 1935).

'Goldtopas'

The cultivar 'Goldtopas' is a low, 40-cm-high multiflowered bedding rose with hybrid tea-type flowers. It was put on the market and patented by the firm of Kordes in 1963. Chosen by the Kordes as parent plants were the

'Goldtopas'

cultivars 'Doctor Faust' (golden-yellow flushed orange and pink) and 'Circus' (yellow, flushed pink and salmon). The cultivar 'Goldtopas' has like characteristics: robust ovoid buds that develop into medium large (8 cm across) flowers coloured yellow-orange with red-orange reverse. They are double and are borne on rather short stalks singly or more often in clusters of several (as many as 10) blooms. The leaves of this cultivar are glossy dark green and healthy.

'Diana'

This 'Diana' is a multiflowered bedding rose developed by the German firm of Tantau, which put it on the market in 1977 and had it patented right away. As in similar instances, the parentage of this variety remains the breeder's secret but floribunda is the category into which it is classed.

It is a rose with globular buds and double, moderately large, medium-yellow flowers with a delicate fragrance and arranged in scant clusters. This is a small upright bush with glossy green, hardy foliage.

40 - 50 cm

'Diana'

Pink multiflowered bedding roses

Pink multiflowered bedding roses, mostly from the Polyantha group, in practice proved best planted in large masses in the parterre of public areas as well as private gardens. If properly cared for they did well in the same site for several decades, e.g. the cultivar 'Joseph Guy' in the chateau courtyard at the world-famous Průhonice park outside Prague.

'Frau Astrid Späth'

The Späth nurseries of Berlin ranked among the best. Before 1930 there suddenly appeared amongst the female parent bushes of the time-tested cultivar 'Joseph Guy' (elsewhere known by the synonym 'Lafayette') a mutant exhibiting a deviation in the form of the flower. This sport was picked out, multiplied, and named in honour of Mme Späth (it should be added that it also appears under the name 'Direktör Rikala'). It is a pure carmine-red, loosely double rose with prominently wavy petals. The blooms are nearly globular in outline and borne in many-flowered clusters. This rose makes a small bush up to 40 cm high, with mat to faintly glossy light to dark green, healthy leaves.

'Cocorico'

The multiflowered floribunda 'Cocorico' was developed by Meilland in southern France in the early 1950s.

It won a gold medal in 1951 in Geneva and from the British RNRS (Royal National Rose Society). The parents of this rose were the carmine 'Alain' and 'Orange Triumph', one of the parents of

'Frau Astrid Späth'

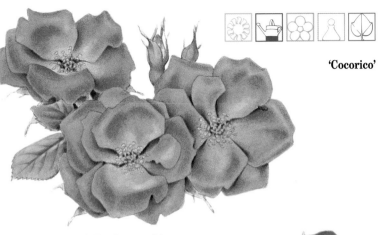

'Cocorico'

the cultivar 'Alain'. The flowers of the new cultivar were large (up to 8 cm across), glowing deep to orange-pink, single to faintly semi-double, with faintly spicy scent, and carried singly but more often in many-flowered clusters. This rose forms an upright bush, taller than usual for multiflowered bedding roses, and has healthy, glossy pale green leaves.

'Fanal'

'Fanal'

To retain one's popularity for 50 years is no mean feat, especially in the face of the competition of tens of thousands of rose cultivars. In 1946 the Tantau nurseries of Holstein introduced in war-devastated Germany a lovely new bedding rose named 'Fanal' and generally classed as a floribunda. It was produced by the pollination of the female parent rose, an unnamed seedling resulting from the crossing of the cultivars 'Johanna Tantau' (white) and 'Heidekind' (pink), with the pollen of the pink shrub rose 'Hamburg'.

The result was a bedding floribunda about 60 cm high with moderately double flowers (less than 20 petals) coloured light red or pink-orange with slightly paler centre and golden-yellow stamens. The flower clusters are usually composed of 10-15 blooms. The foliage is glossy light to dark green, the habit is upright.

Deep red multiflowered bedding roses

Both cultivars shown here have blooms that are a sensational deep red to deep scarlet but both have one and the same handicap - they are susceptible to black spot.

'Marlena'

Gardens designed by me are readily recognised for they always have at least one large bed of these roses. 'Marlena' is one of the best multiflowered bedding roses of all. It was developed by the firm of Kordes and put on the market in 1964; before that (in 1962) as well as later (in 1964, 1966) it won several gold medals at important rose shows. Its parents were the scarlet 'Gertrud Westphal' and the very similar 'Lili Marleen'. The new

'Marlena'

'Puszta'

cultivar had semi-double (18 petals), moderately large flowers, opened out flat in full bloom, arranged in large clusters, and with a long flowering period. It is a small bush about 35-40 cm high with faintly glossy to mat, dark green foliage.

'Puszta'

It is extraordinary how little is known about this cultivar! It is a floribunda, a multiflowered bedding rose, lovely even when the leaves first emerge; these are usually carmine at the beginning, then dark green flushed with purple, and glossy. This cultivar was allegedly developed by the German firm of Tantau about 1972. Called 'Puszta' (sometimes written 'Pussta'), it has fairly large, double, slightly goblet-shaped flowers growing several to a cluster on short stalks. It is a small upright bush reaching a height of up to 70 cm under good conditions.

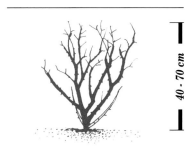

40 - 70 cm

Glowing red multiflowered bedding roses

Low multiflowered bedding roses need not have classic well-formed flowers. They must, however, have a large number of flowers, so many as to give the bed the effect of a monolithic expanse of colour.

'Farandole'

The gold medallist of the 1959 show in Rome was developed by the Meilland company of southern France as the product of two half-siblings: the female parent of both was the deep yellow cultivar 'Goldilocks' and the male parent of one was the pink-red 'Moulin Rouge' and of the other the salmon-pink 'Fashion'. The new cultivar had ovoid buds, glowing red, moderately double flowers (25 petals), opened out flat in full bloom, unscented, but borne in large and full clusters. It is a vigorous (up to 80 cm high), upright, branched bush with mat green foliage.

'Picasso'

The ancestors of this 'Picasso' are extraordinarily diverse: the breeder McGredy first of all crossed Kordes' pink shrub rose 'Frühlingsmorgen' with the cultivar 'Orange Sweetheart'. He had to wait some time to see what would be the result. Then he selected

one of the seedlings whose properties were known only to him and pollinated the scarlet 'Irish Wonder' with its pollen. Then he waited again to see what would come of it. After a time, measurable in years, he again selected one of the seedlings produced by this cross (likewise one whose properties were known only to him) and with its pollen pollinated the well-known multiflowered bedding rose 'Marlena'. This work ended in 1971 when McGredy put on the market the cultivar 'Picasso'. It is a faintly semi-double, cherry-red to glowing red rose. Fully opened blooms have a gleaming white

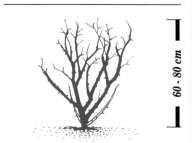

60 - 80 cm

'Farandole'

'Picasso'

centre from which white veins sometimes radiate. The firm of McGredy described the coloration of the flowers as "hand-painted". The flowers are carried in rich, full clusters. It has a bushy, compact habit and height of up to 60 cm, the leaves are small and mat green.

Bicoloured multiflowered bedding roses

The bicolouredness of roses, be they large-flowered or multiflowered bedding roses, may be spatial or time-related. Commonest is colour differentiation of the petals' inner side and reverse, next comes colour toning, transitions from light to dark tones, or transitions of marked contrast. Bicolouredness in terms of time is a difference in colour of flowers of different age (not only length of flowering period); sometimes this diversity is so pronounced that one flower is entirely pink and another entirely yellow.

'Rumba'

'Rumba'

The Danish firm of Poulsen developed one of the brightly coloured "dance" multiflowered bedding roses (in addition to Kordes' 'Samba' these also include Meilland's 'Charleston'). As in similar instances, the parent cultivar was the brightly coloured 'Masquerade' which was pollinated with the pollen of an unnamed seedling, product of the hybridisation of the pink cultivar 'Poulsen's Gruppenrose' and the vermilion-red cultivar 'Floradora'. The dominant influence of the female parent is, of course, indisputable: the ovoid buds develop into brightly coloured golden-yellow to orange flowers flushed with poppy-red. In older flowers, the red tones prevail, late flowers, on the contrary, are practically entirely yellow.

'Woburn Abbey'

'Samba'

'Samba'

Kordes' floribunda 'Samba' is the daughter of 'Rumba', pollinated with the pollen of an unknown seedling. More detailed data is probably the breeder's secret. The buds are globular, the basic colour is golden-yellow edged red; the petals are also red on the reverse. Red to scarlet later totally predominates. The flowers are moderately large, double, slightly reminiscent of large-flowered bedding roses in structure; they are carried in large clusters on short stalks. It has a spreading bushy habit and height of 40-50 cm. The leaves are glossy deep green.

'Woburn Abbey'

Even the English cultivar 'Woburn Abbey' cannot deny that its female parent was the famous 'Masquerade'.

The breeder George Sidey pollinated it with the pollen of the salmon-pink cultivar 'Fashion'. Such parents gave rise to a high-quality multiflowered bedding rose, ornamental not only by virtue of the unusual colour of its flowers but also the attractive dark foliage lasting even in freezing weather. The ovoid buds develop into golden-yellow to orange flowers shaded a darker orange-red. The blooms are large (up to 8 cm), well-formed, later somewhat flat, faintly double, and fragrant. They are carried in airy clusters of several blooms. This rose is particularly effective in full sun; in open situations with a short period of full sunlight it is susceptible to mildew.

Climbing and rambling roses

All roses are light-loving woody plants. This also determines their life strategy: they must know how to find and defend their place in the sun. And so over the centuries they developed three different means of doing so, means that proved so successful that roses have grown in these ways from the Tertiary to this day.

Roses that developed in open spaces, such as steppes, where there was no competition from other woody plants, but where it was necessary to cope with tufted grasses, they chose the strategy of spreading gradually beneath the soil surface. A typical example is the Gallic or French rose

Flowering stem of a climbing rose

(*Rosa gallica*). If there are, say, 5-10 such small rose bushes growing in a hedgerow they are not 5-10 separate individuals but a single individual from a single seed that has grown to form a spreading colony.

Roses that developed amidst shifting rubble or by the waterside likewise had to keep a firm hold on the substrate: these formed compact colonies producing little-branched main stems and numerous but short underground runners. When the rubble broke off with them or they were torn off by ice as it broke up during the spring thaw, the whole clump simply moved a bit farther on, caught hold, and grew.

Worst off were the roses that grew in woodlands enveloped by and faced with the competition of taller shrubs and trees. These could have been completely shaded within a short time and so all they could do was adapt to the given conditions. This they did by developing stout, often hooked thorns and short, thorny twigs growing out from the main stems at a blunt angle. These adaptations served to enable the

'Blossomtime' *(O'Neal and Bosley, 1951)*
is an outstanding climbing rose, offspring
of the famous 'New Dawn'.

roses to reach aloft by thrusting their way up a suitable support, e.g. a strong shrub, or tree. Yes, even the dog rose, which also belongs to this group, is a climber or rambler.

To this group also belong the East Asian roses of the section Synstylae, first and foremost among them *Rosa multiflora*. It is a typical rambler that is capable of sending up a main stem up to 4 m long in a single year. In general it may be said that most roses of the section Synstylae are suitable for breeding climbing roses for the very reason that they have exceedingly long main stems.

Climbing roses are therefore characterised chiefly by the formation of long main stems. The ones that won out were those whose wood tolerated low temperatures even when young; if their wood were damaged by frost and had to be cut back hard they would hardly be able to cover arches and pergolas. The blooms may be like those of large-flowered or like those of multiflowered bedding roses. Some cultivars produce flowers repeatedly, others just once a year. In catalogues they are generally designated by the letters Cl. (climbing), sometimes also together with other letters depending on their derivation, e.g. Cl. HT for climbing roses derived from hybrid teas, Cl. Pol. for roses derived from Polyanthas, and the like.

Roses have been bred and newly developed roses named since the dawn of gardening. Commercialisation in the first half of the 20th century led not only to the concealment of the parentage of new roses but also to the protection of new cultivars and their names. New roses began to be patented: - for the first time in the US in 1930 when the first rose to be thus registered under Patent No. 1 was 'New Dawn'.

'New Dawn'

This is an accidental mutant of the pale pink cultivar 'Dr W. van Fleet', discovered in the beds of the Somerset Rose Nursery in New Brunswick, in the American state of New Jersey. It is an extraordinarily long-flowering (one winter outside Prague it still had flowers on Boxing Day), hardy, healthy, climbing rose with very glossy dark green leaves and double, shell- pink, fragrant flowers of classic, shapely form. The main stems it sends up each year may reach a length of 3 to 4 m.

'Lichtkönigin Lucia'

Many roses put on the market as "shrub" roses are nowadays used as

'New Dawn'

'Lichtkönigin Lucia'

climbing roses. One such is the cultivar shown. In substance it is only a gardening trick whether a vigorous rose is trained up a support or else left to grow naturally and form a bush.

The parents of Kordes' 'Lichtkönigin Lucia' were the yellow cultivar 'Zitronenfalter' (unfortunately we know not which, for there are two of the same name) and Kordes' yellow climbing rose 'Climbing Cläre Grammerstorf' from which it inherited the tendency to produce lengthy main stems. Introduced in 1985, it is a yellow, semi-double (18 petals) rose with reddish stamens. The flowers are carried in loose clusters of 3-5 blooms and are faintly to moderately scented. The main stems are 1.5 to 2 m long and stout, the leaves mat to glossy dark green.

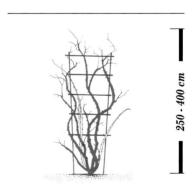

250 - 400 cm

The ability to climb a suitable support is one that was bestowed upon the evolutionary branch of the genus *Rosa* that was able to form hooked thorns. Cultivated climbing roses fulfil this requirement but in addition to a suitable support they also require skilful hands and a good eye on the part of the grower. When the good traits of man and rose are joined, the result can be something wonderful - as the drawings from historic rose gardens in the final chapter testify.

'Meg'

The climbing rose 'Meg' was developed by the English breeder Dr A.C.V. Gosset of Cornborough as early as 1954 by crossing the yellow 'Paul's Lemon Pillar' (whose ancestors include the famous 'Frau Karl Druschki' and 'Marechal Niel') with the pink 'Mme Butterfly'.

'Meg' is a pale pink rose with apricot-yellow centre, with large, semi-double to almost single blooms. The flowers are opened out flat, fragrant, produced in the greatest number in summer, sometimes with a repeat flowering in autumn.

'Meg'

'Clair Matin'

'Clair Matin'

Predominantly a European climber
- European because it and its parents
were developed mostly in Europe - it
was put on the market in 1960 by the
French firm of Meilland of Cap
d'Antibes. Its parentage includes
Kordes' multiflowered bedding rose
'Orange Triumph' and floribunda
'Kordes Sondermeldung', the English
'Phyllis Bide' (from this it probably
inherited its climbing properties), and
the famous American floribunda
'Fashion'.

'Clair Matin' is a delicate pink,
fragrant, semi-double rose with blooms
about 6 cm across, goblet-shaped
to opened out flat, flowering profusely

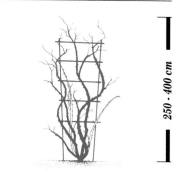

250 - 400 cm

and long. The main stems are up to
3 m long, the leaves healthy,
glossy, leathery. The flowers last a long
time in water even if they are cut in full
bloom.

The mid-20th century marked the appearance, one shortly after the other, of new climbing rose cultivars that at first glance resembled wild roses, for their wide-open flowers rarely had more than 5-7 petals. Nevertheless they made a big splash with their profusion of blooms and lovely colours.

'Cocktail'

Rose-growing is rather a peculiar business. Take, for example, such cultivars as 'Cocktail' and 'Clair Matin'. Apparently this was truly a case of identical crossing but the composition of the offspring was extraordinary. 'Cocktail' was produced according to the following scheme: ('Kordes Sondermeldung' x 'Orange Triumph') x 'Phyllis Bide' and that is precisely the scheme of the male parent of the cultivar 'Clair Matin'. The breeder was likewise the same - Meilland, the only difference is that 'Cocktail' was introduced three years earlier (1957). 'Cocktail' can also be grown in two ways: with a support as a climbing rose, without one as a spreading bush.

The flowers are single or with a few more petals, open, about 6 cm across, carried in rich clusters of many blooms, coloured a conspicuous red with pale centre and faintly scented. The main stems are up to 2 m long, the leaves leathery and glossy dark green.

'Dortmund'

'Dortmund' is one of Kordes' famous roses. It was put on the market in 1955 as the offspring of an unnamed seedling whose flowers had been pollinated with the pollen of *Rosa x kordesii*.

It is a climbing rose with stout main stems up to 3 m long. The flowers are nearly single - with five or slightly more petals coloured blood red with a small white "eye", up to 10 cm across when fully open, and carried in rich clusters of numerous blooms. The foliage is glossy dark green.

'Dortmund' serves as an example of how misleading the classification of roses is, not only of cultivated roses but also of the wild "botanical" ones. And just as we all speak of the dog rose as a shrub, even if it is a rambler, so Kordes himself classed 'Dortmund' as a shrub rose - though with the singular feature that it climbs.

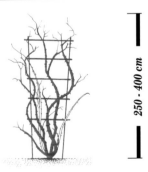

250 - 400 cm

'Cocktail'

'Dortmund'

Miniature roses

The island of Mauritius did not acquire renown only with its famed blue stamp of 1847. Long before that, it was a sort of transfer station for unusual small roses derived from the China rose and called *Rosa chinensis* var. *minima*. It was from there that these roses, small in size as well as blooms, were brought to Europe. This was sometime between 1810 and 1815 and the first European country to grow them was England. The trail ends here for a while.

Some years later it was rumoured that somewhere in Switzerland the country folk grew some sort of tiny rose in pots in the windows of their farmhouses. In the meantime - in 1815 - the English botanist John Sims described a dwarf rose which he named *Rosa semperflores* var. *minima*. It was also known as the "Miss Lawrance Rose". Two years later the Frenchman Redouté drew a different small rose which the Englishman Thory

The foliage of some miniature roses is a perfect ground cover.

named *Rosa indica pumila*, and one year after that (in 1818), another Englishman by the name of Sweet described these small roses from the island of Mauritius as *Rosa lawranceana*.

Shortly after, sometime round 1823, another small rose was offered for sale in pots in Paris markets. This went by the name of Pompon de Paris and soon became established in other European countries as well. It was offered by German gardeners round about 1850.

Soon various mutations appeared on the scene; these were named and described as varieties (cultivars) and so by the close of the 19th century there existed some 50 cultivars. It was not until about 1917 that a Dr Roulett found the fabled miniature Swiss rose at the village of Mauborget in the Swiss canton Jura. Alas, before it was possible to get hold of it the village was destroyed by fire and with it all the roses. Nevertheless after a time it was discovered in a neighbouring village and in 1920 the French gardener

'Margot'

H. Correvon grew it from cuttings taken there and named it *Rosa roulettii,* in honour of the man who found it. However, it turned out that it was nothing other than the earlier French Pompon de Paris.

Many growers tried their hand at selective breeding of miniature roses but the most famous in this respect was the firm of the Dot family of Spain. Currently grown under the name dwarf roses or miniature roses, possibly also rock garden roses, are cultivars truly descended from *Rosa chinensis* 'Minima' as it is now officially called, as well as growth deviations from well-known garden roses, generally Polyanthas - these often bear the English prefix Baby, e.g. 'Baby Masquerade'. In catalogues miniature roses are designated by the letters Min.

Miniature roses are nowadays also sold in pots.

"Small is beautiful", a popular saying goes. And miniature roses are beautiful in their own way, of course. They cannot compete with the regalness of those royal blooms, the large-flowered bedding roses, but they possess something the latter might well envy: they can be, and often are, grown as potted plants and are thus available even to those who must be content with a flower on the table or in the window.

'Perle de Monserrat'

This by now already classic miniature rose could serve as a symbol for the whole class. And not without reason, for it belongs to the "first filial generation" of *Rosa roulettii*. It was developed by the Dot family firm before 1945 and put on the market by the Meillands. The female parent was the tiny pink Polyantha 'Cécile Brunner', cultivated from as far back as 1881, and the pollen was from *Rosa roulettii*.

'Perle de Monserrat' is a rose about 30 cm tall with fine thorns and dark green foliage. The flowers are small, typical of true "roulettii", deep pink in the centre, paler - "pearly pink" - towards the edges, broadly open like a rosette, and carried in scanty clusters of a few blooms.

'Perle de Monserrat'

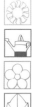

'Perle de Alcañada'

'Perle de Alcañada'

This comes from the same firm, the Dot nurseries in Spain, and is but one of Dot's "pearls". The female parent was the cultivar 'Perle des Rouges', the male parent *Rosa roulettii*. It was introduced in 1944 by the French firm of Meilland. It is a very successful miniature rose, occasionally "lost" under a great many synonyms: 'Baby Crimson', 'Pearl of Canada', 'Wheatcroft's Baby Crimson', etc. The flowers are carmine, very small, semi- double, opened out flat, and carried in rich clusters. It is a small plant, up to 30 cm high, with small, narrow, dark green leaves.

If it were not for the discovery and development of the class of miniature roses descended from *Rosa chinensis* 'Minima', their role would probably have been filled by low-growing, small-flowered, and small-leaved Polyanthas. Typical representatives of these are the cultivars 'The Fairy' and 'Alberich'.

'The Fairy'

The cultivar 'The Fairy' was put on the market by the Englishman F.A. Bentall in 1932. It is a chance mutant of the pink climbing (!) cultivar 'Lady Godiva'. It has small, double, pale pink-red, rosette-shaped flowers (2.5 cm) carried in rich clusters of many blooms. It forms low, broadly spreading bushes up to 50 cm high; the stems are branched, the leaves small and glossy.

'The Fairy'

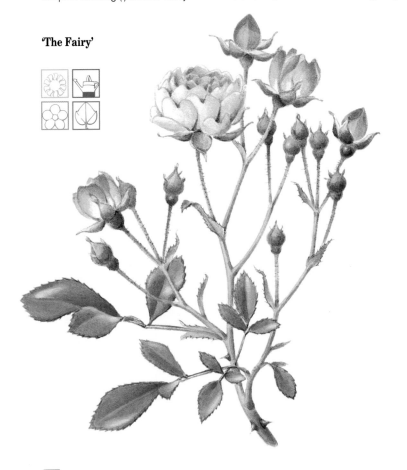

'Alberich'

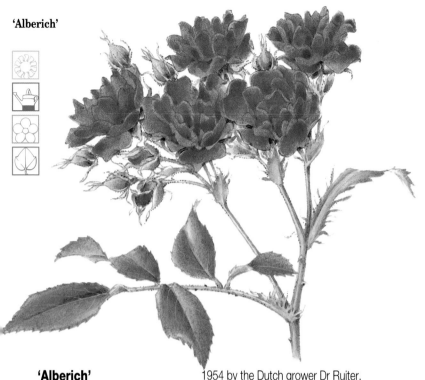

'Alberich'

Also commonly grown, the cultivar 'Alberich' is not a true miniature rose but only a very small-flowered and small-leaved Polyantha. It was developed and put on the market in

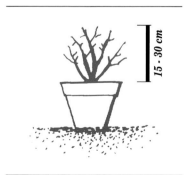

15 - 30 cm

1954 by the Dutch grower Dr Ruiter. The female parent was the cultivar 'Robin Hood' (which one, we wonder, when there are two of the same name!), and the pollen came from a seedling of the cultivar 'Katharina Zeimet' - once again two great unknowns. Nevertheless the result not only exceeded all expectations but also stood the test of time, for 'Alberich' continues to be grown and remains a great favourite (could that be the reason it was called 'Happy' in English-speaking regions and especially in the US?) for low beddings to this day. The flowers are currant-red, semi-double, very small, the leaves glossy dark green. It forms branching bushes rarely taller than 20 cm.

After many years of hybridisation, growers managed to smuggle bicolouredness also into the makeup of miniature roses. Successful in this endeavour was A. Meilland at Cap d'Antibes: in 1958 he put on the market the rose 'Colibri' and after a time (in 1972) 'Shooting Star'.

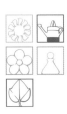

'Shooting star'

'Shooting Star'

The female parent of the cultivar 'Shooting Star' was the bicoloured Polyantha 'Rumba' and the male parent a seedling that was the product of a cross between 'Dany Robin' and 'Perle de Monserrat' (it was the latter that gave this rose its miniature character). The blooms are golden-yellow edged red, double, goblet-shaped and faintly scented (a rare trait in miniature roses!); they are lasting and carried singly or in scant clusters. The small bushes of this cultivar are no taller than 30 cm and the leaves are small and light green.

When one bends down over this little beauty one cannot help wondering

'Colibri'

why the grower named it 'Shooting Star', in other words an object of transient beauty, or was the model another flower, the primula *Dodecatheon*, also known as Shooting Star?

'Colibri'

Because I grew this miniature rose for years myself I know what it is to be captivated by it. The same must have happened to A. Meilland as well because he devoted himself to developing miniature roses with the same intensity he devoted to developing new roses of the other classes. He pollinated the American yellow floribunda 'Goldilocks' with the pollen of the miniature rose 'Perle de Monserrat' and in 1958 named the resulting selected seedling 'Colibri'. The flowers are orange-yellow either flushed or patterned coral-red; the colours fade with age or are paler in late summer blooms. The flowers are small, fairly double, faintly scented, opened out flat,

and carried singly or in large numbers in scanty clusters. The leaves are small, healthy, deep green. However, watch out for a case of mistaken identity, for there exists a yellow Polyantha of the same name dating back to 1898 although this is not grown much nowadays.

20 - 30 cm

Standard roses

Whereas all the preceding types of roses could be classed in readily defined groups with specific characteristics and cultivars that fulfilled the criteria of the respective group, the brief chapter on standard roses steers clear of such criteria for the subject in question concerns a gardening method used not only for roses but for numerous other garden plants. The past decade in particular has witnessed a resurgence in the popularity of this once traditional method of growing plants on a very tall sturdy stem.

Standard rose in a portable container

What is the substance of this method? If a plant is itself sufficiently vigorous and forms sturdy stems, one stout shoot is selected for the purpose and all the sidegrowths on it are removed, leaving only the growing point at the top. As soon as the shoot attains the required height, the growing point is pinched to develop a head.

Nowadays, of course, many plants are grown in this way, even some that were not grown like this before, for practically any plant can be trained to grow in this manner, all except, perhaps, a few such as radish or kohlrabi. To begin with I have seen magnificent fuchsias and pelargoniums as well as the currently fashionable "Paris Chrysanthemums" (*Argyranthemum frutescens*, syn. *Chrysanthemum frutescens*); laurels have been grown thus for centuries, and even forsythias and weigelias look very effective grown as standards. And Bohemia is noted for being the first region to grow gooseberries in the form of standards.

'Golden Medal'

The second method is to select a suitable stem-forming rootstock. Then when it attains the desired height, the cultivar is grafted or budded on at the point where it should develop a head. That is how weeping willows, larches, gooseberries, pelargoniums, fuchsias, and above all roses are grown.

Good as rootstock is any rose that does not have a tendency to form colonies (does not put out underground runners) and whose stems grow upright.

The height of the stems on which the cultivated variety is budded is traditionally about 100-140 cm. This height is determined by a number of factors: one of the important ones is

what cultivar is to be carried by such a stem. The taller the stem, the greater the danger of its uprooting, breaking, and the like. If the cultivar to be budded is a miniature rose (which I strongly recommend), the stem can be shorter and more slender, if the head is formed by a hybrid tea cultivar, the stem must be sturdy and stout. The basic measure of the choice of budded cultivar should be its habit; the choice should thus be a cultivar of compact non-branching habit.

a short stem: such roses are grown as portable, mobile roses, the smallest of which are the bonsai.

Growing standard roses

Growing standard roses, with the exception of the last named, has further singular features: one is overwintering, the other the necessity of keeping the stem upright. If a classic stake is chosen for this purpose, it must be anchored in the ground before the rose is planted. The rose is planted beside it at an angle of about 30 degrees, i.e. at a slight slant, so it can be bent to the ground for the winter and the head protected by covering it with a layer of soil. Other methods consist of constructions of metal or plastic that can be dismounted for the winter.

In recent years classic standard roses have been augmented, particularly in France, by so-called umbrella, or weeping tree roses. The principle is simple: Budded on a tall stem is a suitable climbing rose cultivar. The opposite trend tends towards growing small-flowered cultivars on

A historical rose garden with a combination of standard and climbing roses. In terms of garden design, standard roses are a singular element. If used in large numbers it is necessary to observe the principle of absolutely the same height for every stem. Because this is an element that evolved in the period of the so-called regular, particularly baroque gardens, standard roses can hardly be used in the natural-style garden.

Standard roses: a - on a short stem (60-70 cm), b - on a tall stem (70-100 cm), c - on a stem for weeping tree roses (140-160 cm).

Propagation of roses from seed

Propagation of roses from seed, also termed sexual reproduction, is the basic natural method of ensuring the reproduction of a natural taxon. Roses are normal higher plants and are equipped with the standard reproductive system.

They have bisexual flowers of classic structure, consisting of five sepals, five petals, a large number of stamens with anthers (i.e. the male reproductive organs) and a large number (10 to 40) of pistils (female reproductive organs).

A singular feature of roses is that the pistils grow from a fleshy receptacle that later develops into the hip, which is a false fruit, the true fruits being the achenes inside.

Longitudinal section of hip (left). In the centre of the fleshy hip are the true fruits, achenes, surrounded by hairs that prick the skin when cutting the hip open. Right - enlarged achene.

The way the pistils grow from the receptacle is an important distinguishing characteristic, used in determining to which of the species of the genus Rosa a rose belongs, as is the number of styles, their indumentum (hairiness or glabrousness) and similar characteristics. In some roses, the styles are joined to form a sort of column that juts far beyond the top of the hip: such roses belong to the section Synstylae and played a significant role in the development of modern garden roses, as I already mentioned in the preceding chapters.

In most other roses the styles are loose and form a low, appressed head or a ragged "posy" of sorts at the top of the hip.

Development of the fruits

Following pollination, the fertilised ovules in the ovaries develop into the true fruits - one-seeded achenes. These are the tiny stones inside the hips mistakenly believed by many to be seeds. They are extraordinarily hard and difficult to split open; they consist of two

*'Elysium' (Kordes 1961) is
a multiflowered bedding rose of the
F group.*

halves joined by a sort of seam of hemicellulose.

Hemicellulose is an organic compound easily decomposed by the digestive juices of some animals, which leads to better germination of the seeds. For that reason growers of rootstock roses feed the achenes to pigs, removing them from the pigs' dung afterwards and sowing them in the ground. They say germination is greatly speeded up by this. They're probably right, because unless they are harvested at the right time, the achenes of roses will not sprout the year they are sown but will remain dormant and will not germinate until a year later. That, of course, means a great financial loss to large nurseries who are in the business to make money. This late germination forms part of a strategy roses use,

which includes a "germination rest period".

Nurserymen, who annually require thousands of rootstock roses (and the easiest and cheapest way to obtain these is by sowing seeds), as well as breeders, for whom every single achene produced by hybridisation is important (for what if one of them were to give rise to a new cultivar that would make them famous!), therefore seek various methods of inducing roses to germinate already the first year after the seeds are harvested.

Apart from the unaesthetic and not very appealing method discussed earlier, using the pig as an intermediary, there is another way of disrupting the germination rest period: using the method known as stratification.

Stratification

The achenes of roses harvested at the right time should never be allowed to dry out. After being extracted from the hips (be careful the hairs inside the hips do not get under your shirt collar or into your cleavage when doing so - at one time they were used to make a famous "itching powder" - you'll find out what that means only too soon if you try it) and while they are still moist they are put in a suitable container (pot, pan) on a thick layer of damp sand and covered with a further layer of sand. There may be several such layers in a single pot or pan. The container is then put in a cool and damp place (e.g. a cellar), or it may be dug into the ground in the garden. Early in spring the container is taken up, the achenes and sand are separated with care, and the achenes are sown in the usual way. They germinate in darkness and should therefore be covered with a layer of soil the same thickness as the achenes.

If you decide to put the container with the stratified achenes into the ground in the garden, cover it with a thick mesh or a brick so mice cannot get at the achenes. Otherwise you're in for an unpleasant surprise in spring in the form of a sand-filled pot with which you can at most make mud pies.

Ludvík Večeřa of Průhonice outside Prague once hit upon another method, one based on stratification: he "sowed" the achenes right after they were harvested into a mixture of sand and soil in a cool greenhouse and kept them at a temperature of about 5 °C from autumn throughout the whole winter. Sometime at the end of February he turned the heat on in the greenhouse (under the window ledge) and the achenes germinated so readily that the roses that grew from them bore flowers that very same year.

The period of rest before germination can be disrupted in other ways as well: by soaking in hot and cold water, by the action of acids, or by so-called scarification, scraping or cutting the hard pericarp. The last-named method has its drawbacks in that the incipient rose may be damaged mechanically.

Harvesting

Another way to get around the germination problem is to harvest at the

Stratification of the fruits of a hip. The achenes are placed in a flowerpot on a layer of damp sand on top of a thin layer of gravel and then covered with damp sand; when stratifying larger quantities of achenes, several layers may be put in the container.

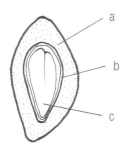 

*Scarification of achenes: left - longitudinal section of an achene
(a - hard pericarp, b - seed, c - embryo); right - diagram of a cut made when
scarifying to release the seed without damaging the embryo.*

right time: some rose growers claim that the best time is when the hips have attained their full size but are still green, with perhaps just the first flush of red. At that stage the achenes are not yet completely hardened and germinate as soon as sown. A method that others have found successful is to leave the hips on the shrub until after the first frost, which softens them.

This, however, does not hold true should you decide to obtain offspring from one of the loveliest wild roses, the East Asian *Rosa roxburghii*, or use it for hybridising. Its hips look like small horse chestnuts still enclosed in their green prickly burs. The hips of this rose are similarly spiny but unbelievably hard. To get at the achenes, I pounded them with a hammer with all my strength - but to no avail. In the end I just had to leave them in the ground to rot, which in its way was a form of stratification.

One thing is certain, a germination rest period is typical of all roses and greatly complicates the work not only of those who grow roses for sale but that of hybridisers and breeders as well.

Hybridisation

The great majority of cultivated roses were produced by hybridisation. In the case of single roses there is no problem with preparing the flowers in time, i.e. removing the male organs (stamens) from the female parent plants. This is necessary because roses are largely autogamous and are pollinated by their own pollen. The only way to have certainty about the transfer of the traits of the male parent is to remove the stamens with their anthers in time (i.e. while still in the unopened bud).

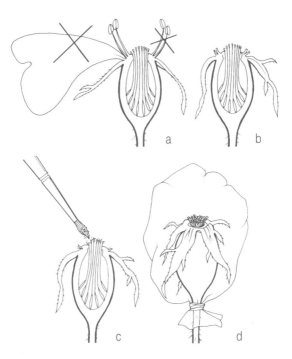

Hand pollination of roses: a, b - removal of petals and stamens (anthers), c - transfer of pollen from another plant with a brush, d - enclosing the flower in a cheesecloth bag or nylon stocking.

Pollen from plants selected as male partners is transferred with a brush to the stigmas of flowers that have just opened. In the case of double flowers, sterilisation by the timely removal of stamens is more difficult, nevertheless it is a must for intentional hybridisation.

Propagation of roses from seed is used when growing rootstock roses and in hybridisation when seeking new varieties. The multiple hybrids of today's modern roses produce offspring of such diversity that there is not the slightest hope of their being reproduced by this method. That is why it is necessary to propagate them by vegetative means.

Propagation of roses from seed often came up against other obstacles as well. In some groups of roses meiosis is not regular (meiosis is a term used in genetics denoting a phase in the differentiation of chromosomes). During this process, in normal plants with regular meiosis the number of chromosomes is somatically halved so that the normal number is again restored following the fusion of the male and female gametes (mature germ cells). However, such is not the case in roses with irregular meiosis; their male gametes always carry only seven chromosomes and the female gametes carry a somatic number divided not by two but by seven. In hybridisation this sometimes resulted in the production of plants whose further generations were sterile, thus complicating the work of hybridisers.

Rose seedlings

Rose seedlings have all the characteristics of dicotyledonous plants. The cotyledons are entire, the first true leaves are also still undivided, but the second leaves may already be composed of three leaflets. At this stage the seedlings should be pricked out into taller pots from which they may then be moved directly to their permanent site or to a nursery bed. The root systems are deep from the first; when the seedlings are being pricked out, the main root should be shortened by pinching it off.

It is ideal for the healthy and rapid development of the seedlings to put them in open ground as early as possible. If, however, they are to undergo further handling, such as further transfer, it is better to plant them in modules - special compartmentalised peat or plastic trays. The advantage of this is the possibility of transplanting them at any time, the disadvantage the

slowing down of their growth because roses like plenty of room - above as well as below the surface. If, then, you have sown the seeds of some cultivar and are curious about the outcome or if you have gone in for intentional hybridisation, I would recommend the first method - planting in open ground.

Rose seedling: it is pricked out in the first true leaf stage. The main tap root is shortened at the same time.

Vegetative propagation of roses

Vegetative propagation of roses is the only means of preserving and reproducing all the characteristics of the given cultivar (parent plant). In the wild this type of reproduction was taken care of by roses that form spreading colonies, sections of which might be carried off by rubble or water. Sometimes a branch of the dog rose bush arched all the way to the ground, got covered by soil, and took root. That was probably what inspired early gardeners to try doing so on purpose. This method, called layering, was not very successful in the case of roses. Another, similar, method, did work well, however. This was the propagation of plants by cuttings.

Preparing cuttings

A cutting consists of a length of an annual shoot with two or more leaves (and buds in their axils) severed from the female parent plant. In the case of roses, so-called tip cuttings are most successful, i.e. the terminal sections of the current year's semi-ripened shoots or flowering branches pulled off together with a so-called heel, a sliver of the older branch from which it was pulled.

The ideal substrate for cuttings used to be a mixture of one part sharp, washed river sand and one part peat.

'Rémy Martin'

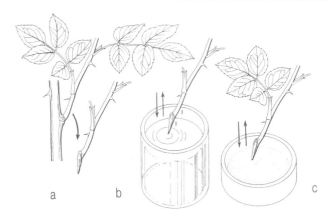

Propagation by semi-hardwood cuttings is carried out in late spring or early summer (June): a - young (current year's) short branches are pulled off an older branch together with a heel, b - they are immersed in clean water, c - then they are dipped into a growth-stimulating powder so the powder clings to the moistened bottom section.

Propagation procedure

Prepared cuttings are first immersed at the base into clean water and then dipped into a growth-stimulating powder. After this a hole is made in the substrate with a slender peg and the cutting is carefully inserted into the hole and firmed in place by pressing the peg into the soil immediately next to the cutting. To prevent possible attack by fungi or bacteria it is recommended to water the cutting with a faintly pink solution of potassium permanganate or camomile extract diluted with water. The adequately moist (but not soggy) substrate with the inserted cuttings is then covered with polythene film stretched taut over wire arches. The best time for this method of propagation by cuttings is late May and June.

Cuttings are carefully inserted into the substrate and polythene film supported by wire arches is stretched over everything.

Propagation by hardwood cuttings

Some rose cultivars can also be successfully propagated by hardwood cuttings, mature ripened stems without leaves, which are severed in the usual way or cut from an older branch along with a small piece of the previous year's wood. Propagating roses by hardwood cuttings is the same as for other woody plants: the cuttings may be taken already before the winter frosts and stored in a bundle in a damp cellar.

Budding

Budding has been the commonest method of the vegetative propagation of roses for over a century. A bud is a tightly closed immature embryo shoot that develops on the plant already in the first half of the preceding summer. Even then it already contains the differentiated basic tissues of the new main stem. Buds are located in the axils of the current year's leaves and are clearly visible only after the leaves have fallen.

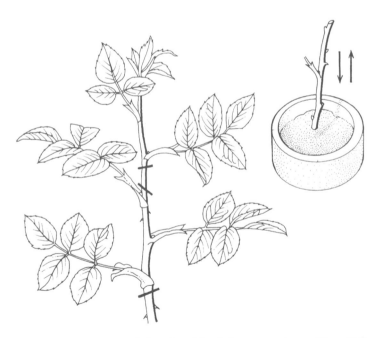

Points for taking late summer stem cuttings. Before planting they are treated with a growth stimulant, like semi-hardwood cuttings.

Buds are prepared for budding when they begin to acquire a reddish tinge. This usually starts in late July but most of it happens in August. First of all selected shoots with well-developed buds are cut off the female parent plant, the thorns are then broken off and with a sharp budding knife a bud is sliced off, with a thin shield-shaped piece of bark attached. Any wood remaining on the underside of the "shield" must be removed. Next, the surface above the neck of the selected stock is carefully cleaned and a T-shaped incision is made in the stem; the two triangular flaps of the incision are gently prised apart (like the lapels of a suit). Then the correctly positioned bud is slipped into this incision and bound firmly with raffia or nowadays more commonly with plastic grafting tape.

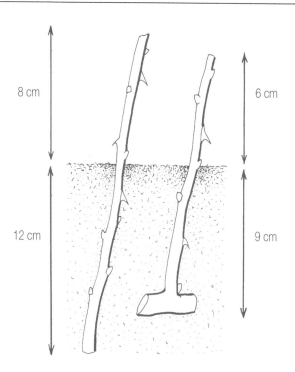

8 cm

6 cm

12 cm

9 cm

Hardwood cuttings of roses may be a section of stem taken at some point along the stem (left) or taken with a piece of older branch (right). They are planted deeper than summer (softwood) and semi-hardwood cuttings.

In addition to classic budding with a so-called winter or dormant bud, occasionally an active bud is still used. This is done in May on plants in the greenhouse where they are already in full growth at that time.

Buds with leaf stalk

It is recommended to take buds from the parent plant together with a leaf stalk, cut off beneath the first pair of leaflets (i.e. above the stipules). Firstly this makes it easier to handle (it can be held by the stalk), secondly it will ensure correct positioning of the bud, and lastly the stalk will serve as a test of the bud's taking power: if the bud has taken well, the remainder of the stalk will fall by itself or at a light touch after 2-3 weeks.

If the bud has not taken, the stump of the stalk remains firm and will not fall.

Forket's method or chip budding

Forket's is a special method of budding. This is done by loosening a piece of bark by cutting downward on the stock, shortening and shaping the bark towards the base to form a tongue, and inserting the bud with shield of the same dimensions behind the tongue. The bud must protrude above the tip of the "tongue". The bud is then tied in with raffia and wax or with plastic tape. This method is used chiefly for budding standard roses and may be carried out practically all year round.

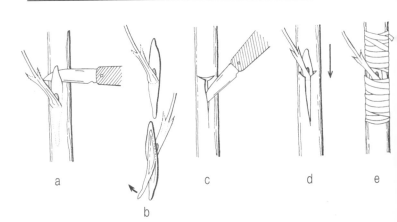

Classic budding of roses: a - slicing the bud from the stem, b - removing remnants of wood, c - making a T-shaped incision, d - slipping the bud into the incision, e - binding the bud firmly.

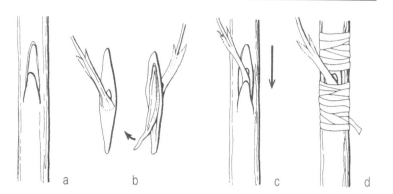

Forket's method of budding: a - special cut down the stem of the stock for Forket's budding, b - bud removed in standard manner and removal of wood, c - inserting the bud, d - binding the bud firmly.

Care of rootstock

After the work of budding has been completed, earth is lightly drawn up around the base of the stock so the bud is level with the surface. After checking that the bud has taken, the binding material can be loosened on the side opposite the bud. The following spring the drawn-up earth is levelled and the stock growth above the bud is cut off at a slight angle: the lower side of the cut should be on the side opposite the bud (so water does not run down into the bud).

Grafting

Another classic method of propagating roses by vegetative means is grafting, either using forced herbaceous (green) scions or woody scions in winter. The methods are the same as in fruit growing, the most common methods being slit or notch grafting followed by whip grafting.

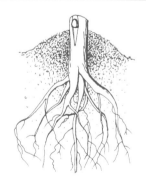

Drawing up earth around the base of the stock and cutting off the stock growth above the bud.

Planting roses

In the previous chapters mention was made of the fact that roses like plenty of sun. In shade they do poorly, are susceptible to disease, mainly fungal diseases, and bear few flowers. That is why the main condition for success in growing roses - no matter what kind - is a suitable, sunny site. Of course it should not have too much sun, such as a bed by the south side of a building. The ideal site appears to be a gentle slope facing east or southeast, less favourable is a situation facing west or south, and least suitable of all is one that faces north.

There should not be any tall trees near a rose bed, particularly ones that have strong root systems with which the roses would have to compete - e.g. ash trees and birches.

The ideal soil for garden roses is humus-rich, sandy loam, though many roses will grow in heavier soils or in loess. The vast majority of roses does well in neutral to mildly alkaline soil. They do not like acid soil but can also be grown there, at least for a time.

Among other things the pH also affects the availability of certain vital elements, lack of which may make itself felt later on the plants' growth, vitality and other aspects.

In view of the fact that many roses are lime-loving plants it is recommended, especially in the case of more acid substrates, to lime the soil regularly.

As a rule, roses have fairly deep roots, but their root systems are sparse (this, of course, applies to cultivated garden roses grown on European *Rosa*

rugosa rootstocks, because the root systems of roses of the section Cinnamomeae and *Rosa gallica* are shallow). That is why the soil must be thoroughly prepared before the planting of garden roses.

If the soil is sufficiently deep, the ideal method of preparing it is trenching, i.e. deep digging to a depth of two spades and good prior application of nutrients. This may be in the form of well-rotted cow manure dug in to a depth of about 30 cm, or ground limestone and suitable phosphate fertiliser. If manure is not available, compost, which is otherwise put on the bottom of the holes when planting, can be used instead.

An element of good soil for roses that is not to be overlooked is a sufficient supply of decomposed organic matter, i.e. humus. Well-decomposed organic matter is proof of the effectiveness of soil organisms and thereby of the "fitness" and nutrient content of the soil. It is thus all to the

'Händel' *(McGredy, 1965) -*
large-flowered climbing rose

good if the soil can be enriched with humus-forming material sufficiently in advance of planting; in addition to strawy manure and compost this may also be leaves raked up in the autumn, grass cuttings, and similar organic refuse from the garden. Of course, care must be taken not to dig in infected plants and plant parts, primarily the leaves of roses affected by black spot, rust, mildew, and the like.

While on the subject of organic refuse such as grass cuttings, it should be noted that many gardeners recommend mulching the soil round newly planted roses with grass cuttings, at least in the beginning.

If such a mulch is later dug in, it is certain to enrich the soil. Nevertheless I tend to rely on experienced rose growers and favour the opinion of the outstanding Czech botanist Dr Deyl, who years ago stated that hoeing twice is equal to fertilising once. That is why I prefer leaving the ground round rose bushes open and hoeing it more often. This results in a better exchange of gases in the soil, better penetration of moisture, and last but not least it disrupts the peaceful life of pests and the germs of various diseases.

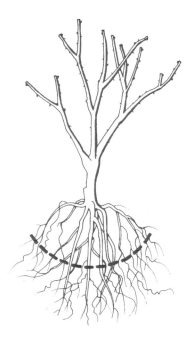

The root system of purchased seedlings should be shortened before planting.

Planting distances

Very good, as a rule, is the so-called triangular spacing where the distance between the bushes of multiflowered bedding roses is about 30-40 cm, both between the individual bushes and between the individual rows; in the case of large-flowered bedding roses the spacing should be 40-50 cm. Miniature roses are generally planted as solitary specimens (in the rock garden), shrub roses require the same amount of space as all large shrubs, and standard roses are generally planted at distances somewhat greater than the height of the stem (so as to leave enough room for them to be bent to the ground for the winter), or else their positioning is determined by the plans of the landscape gardener.

For a flat expanse of bedding roses it is also a good idea to figure out the required number of seedlings. In general for dense plantings of multiflowered bedding roses (with a spacing of 30-40 cm) 9-12 bushes are required for every square metre of soil, for similar dense plantings of large-flowered bedding roses the required number is 7-8 bushes. If miniature roses are used as a ground cover, it is recommended to plant at least 16 seedlings per square metre; in the case of other carpeting varieties, 8-10 seedlings should suffice.

When to plant

Even though the rose is

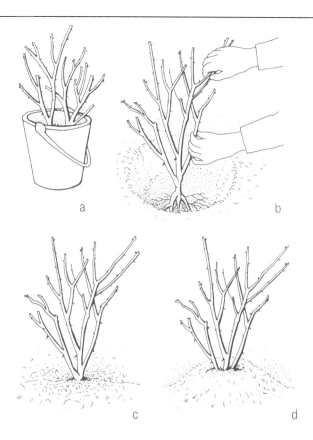

Planting a rose: a - soaking the roots in a thin loamy mush, b - positioning the bush in the hole, c - filling the hole with soil and firming it down, d - drawing up earth around the base - only when planting in autumn!

a deciduous woody plant that can be planted in spring as well as in autumn, autumn planting is definitely better, if only because most growers lift roses from the nursery bed in the autumn and heel in the ones that are not sold. How such heeled-in roses survive the winter - which mainly comes down to whether or not they dry out - depends primarily on the attention devoted to their care.

The best time for planting is the short period from mid-October to mid-November, possibly a few days later.

Roses sold in containers can be planted out at any time during the entire growing period.

First of all dig a hole about 30-40 cm deep and 30-40 cm wide for every bush rose. On the bottom of the hole make a small mound of "better" soil, compost, and the like. Trim the roots by cutting them back with sharp secateurs and remove all damaged and bruised sections that might later rot.

When purchased, rose seedlings should be devoid of leaves. If the leaves were not removed at the nursery or at the shop pull them off yourself as soon as possible (at the latest before planting) and burn them immediately so as not to introduce any fungal diseases to the garden.

Depth of planting

The depth of planting is of particular importance. The seedling must not be planted too deep ("submerged"), nor too shallow (with the roots showing). The point where the rose was budded (bud union) should be slightly beneath the soil surface. Right after the rose is planted, the parts above soil level should be cut back, but only a little; definitive pruning is not carried out until early spring, after the winter is over.

Standard roses, which are often bent to the ground for the winter, are planted in a somewhat different way: they are not planted perpendicular to the supporting stake but at a slight angle of about 30 degrees. The reason for this is to allow the rose to be bent to the ground for overwintering without danger of the part of the stem on which the cultivated rose is budded breaking off.

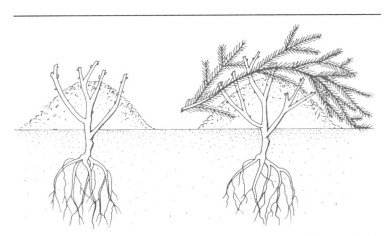

Readying planted-out roses for the winter: left - earthing-up, right - additional protective cover of evergreen boughs. Older plantings are also provided with winter protection in this manner.

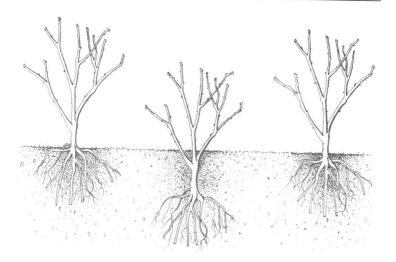

Planting roses: left - too shallow, the neck is above the soil surface; centre - too deep; right - correct depth.

Earthing-up

Before the onset of severe winter frosts, planted roses must be earthed up, i.e. earth must be drawn up round the base. In the case of older plantings, the earth between the bushes is turned over onto the bushes with a spade so it forms a small mound around the base; in the case of newly planted roses it has proved beneficial to put well-rotted compost or good garden soil round the base. The compost or soil is brought to the site in a wheelbarrow; about a spadeful per bush is sufficient.

Heeling-in

If for some reason roses cannot be planted in the autumn they should be heeled in. To heel in roses (as well as other bushes), make a trench in a suitable bed and lay the seedlings into the trench at a slight angle close beside each other and deeper than they will later be in their permanent site. Then cover them with soil, trample this down lightly, and top this with another layer of soil about 25 cm thick. Only the tips of the annual shoots, at most 20 cm long, should be visible above the surface.

Standard roses are heeled in in a dry (!) and shaded spot in a deeper long trench in which they are laid flat (!) and covered with a layer of soil up to 25 cm thick along their entire length. The soil must not be trampled at the spot where the head is, so as not to damage the head.

Routine care of roses

The only sort of plant care people provide automatically, without being taught, is watering; the reason probably is that plants immediately react to lack of water by wilting, whereas neglect in other respects becomes evident only after a certain time.

Watering

Most roses are very well adapted to temporary lack of moisture and therefore even watering of cultivated roses need not be so liberal and regular as, for instance, for cabbage. Nevertheless, roses require sufficient water: the optimum amount roses obtain naturally outdoors is in districts with an annual precipitation of 700-800 mm. In districts where it rains less or in drier years it is necessary to compensate for the possible deficit. Roses need the most water when growth starts in spring and then when they form so-called midsummer shoots, roughly after the first flowers are spent.

Sufficient water must be provided also after every application of fertiliser. Because roses have fairly deep roots, it is necessary to supply the bottom layers of soil with sufficient water - it is best to water at greater intervals but liberally. The optimum amount is about 30 to 50 litres of water for every square metre - at approximately two-week intervals. It is advisable to water the surface of the soil or supply water directly to the roots and let it soak in so the leaves remain dry.

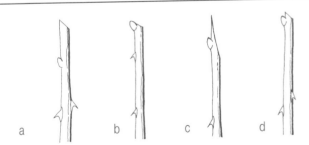

Pruning roses: a - the cut has been made too far away from the bud, b - the cut has been made too close to the bud, c - the cut is too long and may not heal properly, d - the right way to prune: the cut is sloping, starting slightly above the bud and finishing approximately level with the bud opposite to it.

'Kardinal' (Krause 1934), hybrid tea rose

In late summer and autumn, watering should be greatly restricted in order to stop growth and allow the wood to ripen - however do not forget that immediately before the onset of winter when the leaves have already been shed but the soil is not yet frozen, the rose bed should be watered liberally once more.

Weeding

Roses growing in the wild are sufficiently strong to compete successfully with other plants in their vicinity. However, cultivated roses growing in beds are greatly bothered by weeds and in addition to that such beds provide a favourable environment for various pests and incipient rose diseases. Regular weeding of rose beds is the best thing one can do for roses because it generally goes hand in hand with loosening of the soil and improvement of the soil conditions, enables the exchange of gases between the soil and the atmosphere, and also allows better absorption of water, either rainwater or from a watering can.

When the grower wishes to obtain better-quality terminal blooms, it is recommended to break or cut off side blooms in the bud stage. As a rule, miniature roses are not pruned, dried shoots are merely removed - on occasion bushes are cut back en bloc by one half to two thirds their height with garden shears.

Pruning

Pruning is an important procedure in growing cultivated roses, a procedure that should be carried out every year, sometimes even twice a year. The first time is after planting, when the shoots of the seedlings are cut back in spring to 3-5 buds. Each cut must be at the right level and at the right angle, in other words not too far away from the bud, not too close, and not too long. The right cut starts several mm above the bud and finishes opposite to and at least 1-2 mm above the bud.

Early spring pruning

Bedding roses, both large-flowered and multiflowered, are regularly cut back every year in early spring, always leaving about 3-5 active buds on the shoot. Shrub roses always benefit from classic thinning: every year 1-3 older main stems are removed - cut off about 10 cm from the ground. At the same time, if need be, several (not all) shoots are cut back lightly by as much as one third. Climbing roses are pruned

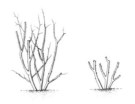

Winter pruning of bedding roses: left - before, right - after pruning.

only after the protective winter covering has been removed: generally, particularly in younger individuals, only the terminal frost-damaged sections of the main stems above the last active bud are cut back, older specimens are thinned in the same way as shrub roses, i.e. the oldest main stems are cut back close to the soil surface. When pruning climbing roses, it is recommended to untie them from the support, spread them out on the ground, and then thin them. Standard roses are shortened in the same way as bedding roses.

Summer pruning

Few growers think of summer pruning, carried out during the growing period. Generally it is restricted to the removal of parts with spent flowers. However, they should not be cut back too hard (at most to the third leaf below the flower) because otherwise the rose would be too weakened. If this pruning were omitted, the rose would start forming fruits, resulting not only in a general weakening of the plant but also in a lesser likelihood of its producing new blooms. It is also necessary to remove the suckers, sprouts growing from the base of the plant, from the point beneath the bud union where the cultivated rose is joined to the rootstock. Such suckers are readily recognised by the difference in shape and colour of the leaves. They should be cut off from the root below the surface of the soil right at the point where they emerge.

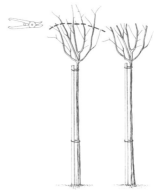

Winter pruning of shrub roses: the main regeneration pruning is carried out on selected main stems close to the ground, shaping pruning is carried out only as required, and only in the head.

The head of standard roses can be shaped by pruning mainly in winter. The head is pruned in a mild curve.

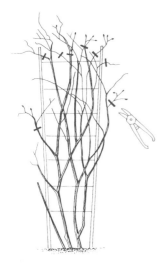

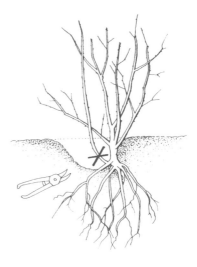

Climbing roses are pruned after the winter by removing only the frost-damaged tips of annual shoots.

Watch out for suckers! Shoots growing from the rootstock must be cut off in time, directly at their point of origin, even if it is below ground.

Overwintering

For most bedding roses the same protection will suffice for the winter i.e. earthing-up - drawing up earth around the base or forming a mound of compost instead. To protect them from the effect of the spring sun it is recommended to cover them with evergreen plants, best of all spruce boughs. Spruce boughs also provide good protection for climbing roses - from the warming rays of the winter or early spring sun rather than from frost. It is also recommended to wrap spruce boughs round the stems of standard roses bent to the ground for the winter. The actual head of the standard rose should never be wrapped, whether with plastic film or some other wrapping. It is still considered best to bend the rose to the ground and cover the head with soil.

Feeding

Roses are woody plants that bear flowers on the current year's wood. For that reason they must expend enormous energy every year into forming flower-bearing branches. And because every year they are deprived of part of their new growth by regular pruning (not to mention roses grown exclusively for cutting) they should be constantly supplied with sufficient food for their hungry stomachs. In many countries special fertilisers for roses are available. If this is not the case, it is necessary to use commercial inorganic fertilisers. In early spring, apply mixed fertilisers in doses of about 60-80 grams per square metre, scattered over the whole area. As soon as buds appear, roses should be given another application of the same fertiliser, but only around the base of each plant; this is repeated once again at the end of

A climbing rose should be protected from the sun's rays in winter and early spring with spruce boughs.

The heads should never be enclosed in polythene, wrapping paper, or similar materials.

June, when the first flowering is finished.

Roses, being fairly lime-loving plants, will appreciate an occasional application of ground limestone (about 0.5 kg/m^2). They do not tolerate potassium fertilisers with a high concentration of chlorine very well and, finally, nitrogenous fertilisers should not

be applied after the first of August (so that roses stop vigorous growth, ripen, and are not damaged by frost). Instead they can be given an additional autumn application of potassium sulphate (30 g/m^2) or phosphate fertilisers (likewise 30 g/m^2).

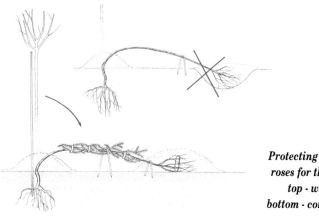

Protecting standard roses for the winter: top - wrong way, bottom - correct way.

Rose pests and diseases

Though considered to be among the hardiest plants, not even wild roses are immune to disease. Cultivated roses, however, are attacked far more by various diseases and pests. The diseases are very often physiological (too little or too much of a certain element, insufficient light, too much water, damage by frost) or may be caused by a pathogen, whether virus, bacteria, fungus, or animal.

In the following pages you will learn about the commonest rose pests and diseases, though there are many more of them than we will discuss here, including viruses, viral mosaic, viral wilting, etc. So far it has been almost impossible to stamp them out; if they do appear care must be taken not to spread them mechanically (with a knife, for instance, or with secateurs) and provide roses with preventive care against sucking insects that could also transmit the viral diseases.

Viral diseases are difficult to control even in humans - even if we are dealing with an ordinary flu virus, let alone an organism like HIV. Of course, in a way, roses are much easier to deal with: a plant infected by a virus should be immediately destroyed - burned. Even composting affected plant remains is advised against.

Many pathogens are highly specialised, for instance, rose mildew and black spot affect only roses. Such specialisation is not as common in the case of pests and many of them are polyphagous and feed on many other plants as well. The range of common pests, chiefly insects, is very wide, ranging from thysanopterous, heteropterous and homopterous insects to hymenopterous insects, beetles, butterflies, and moths.

To date, unfortunately, the most effective protection from pests are chemical preparations: fungicides against fungal diseases, acaricides against mites, and insecticides against insects. Nowadays every country has its regulations determining which preparations are permitted to be used to protect plants and therefore it is impossible to recommend any specific ones in this context. An effective weapon, of course, is prevention, good nourishment of the roses, regular inspections and mechanical (hand) removal of parts of plants showing signs of attack by a fungal disease, bacteria, and the like.

Insufficient development of the upper leaves may be due to a physiological cause or an insect pest.

Another possible deterring factor is the introduction of ladybirds to curb aphids, and similar means of biological control; very effective in the greenhouse, for instance, is the parasitic insect of the genus *Encarsia* that is capable of destroying a whole population of whitefly.

Experienced gardeners advise against mulching the soil round roses, for the plant material is a hotbed of disease, primarily rose mildew and black spot that attack mainly annual shoots.

An effective weapon in the control of pests and diseases is also the agreement of a wider circle of neighbours on a common plan of action, for untreated roses in just a single garden may be a source of infection for all other treated roses in the vicinity.

Diseases of the stems

A very common disease of stems is the one caused by the parasitic fungus *Cylindrosporium ramicola*; it appears as black spots, 3 to 12 mm large, on one-year shoots that are still green. The centres of the spots ultimately become corky, turn brown, the edges reddish. The remedy is immediately cutting off the affected part; a good preventive measure is spraying with a suitable fungicide.

On stems and branches, small spots often appear that later become larger, coloured red to light brown edged violet; in the final stage entire branches die. This is caused by the fungus *Coniothyrium wernsdorffiae*. The remedy is immediate removal and burning of the affected branch. On a stouter branch it is sometimes sufficient to cut out the affected spot and spread grafting wax over the wound.

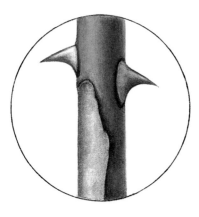

Spots caused on the stem by the fungus Coniothyrium wernsdorffiae.

Diseases of the roots

Roots are prone to the appearance of furrowed tumours on the roots and neck, caused by the bacterium *Agrobacterium tumefaciens*. Affected parts or bushes must be cut out and burned. A possible preventive measure is immersing the roses before planting in a loamy mush with an admixture of dissolved mercury mordant.

Diseases of the leaves

Leaves probably suffer the most. A very common physiological disease is so-called chlorosis, marked by yellowing or rather blanching of the leaves. This is a sign primarily of an iron deficiency, sometimes also of soil that is too alkaline or too acid, possibly also containing too much water. Iron deficiency can be corrected by watering with a 1% solution of iron sulphate or else with special fertilisers.

Various leaf spots and damage is caused also by too small or too large amounts of other elements. If there is too much calcium in the soil, or if the soil is too acid or excessively wet over a long time, these cause physiological chlorosis, when the leaves start to turn yellowish until they are finally entirely yellowish green to whitish yellow with only the areas alongside the ribs remaining green.

If the leaf edges turn yellow and brown and at the same time often curl downward, if the internodes are shorter, and if the buds are few and do not open, all this is due to the presence of chlorine; treatment consists of applying potash fertilisers without chlorine.

Deformation of the leaves, when they acquire all sorts of irregular shapes and the tips curl to form a sort of hood, is caused by a virus and is incurable. Though this disfigures the rose it does not weaken it to a marked degree.

If the leaf tips and edges become dry, this may be due not only to too much water (as in houseplants) but also to a potassium deficiency in the soil.

Magnesium (Mg) deficiency reveals itself by blanching of the leaves along the median rib.

Iron deficiency (so-called chlorosis) reveals itself by yellowing of the leaf edges.

Sometimes you may notice that the leaves of your roses are acquiring a pronouncedly red hue. This need not be only when they are emerging. The cause is low temperatures when, as gardeners say, the roses caught a chill. And since one cannot very well put a scarf round their necks there is no way this can be prevented.

Leaves turning red at low temperatures is not caused by some pathogen. It is a natural process when the plant pigments called anthocyanins act as filters of excessive radiation (something like tanning from exposure to the sun) and are furthermore probably involved also in the plants' mechanisms of resistance to cold, frost, and drought.

Rose mildew

Rose mildew, *Sphaerotheca pannosa* var. *rosae*, is one of the most prevalent of the rose diseases. Varieties with smooth glossy leaves are more prone to this disease than ones with leathery leaves. The occurrence and development of mildew is promoted by insufficient light, humid air with poor circulation, sudden changes in temperature, too much feeding with nitrogen, insufficient potassium, mulching, and soils that are too light and cold.

Protection from mildew

The best way to protect roses from mildew is spraying with sulphur preparations and special fungicides. Plants should be sprayed preventively once every two weeks from June till September. In the autumn it is necessary to remove and burn fallen leaves and affected annual shoots.

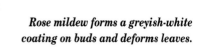

Rose mildew forms a greyish-white coating on buds and deforms leaves.

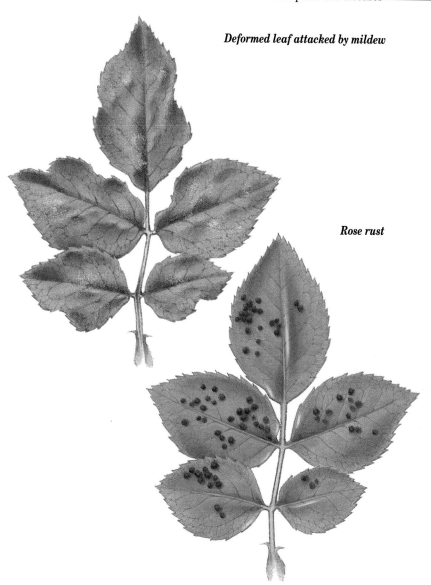

Deformed leaf attacked by mildew

Rose rust

Rose rust

Rose rust, *Phragmidium mucronatum*, attacks roses only occasionally. In spring it forms, mostly on the undersides of the leaves, powdery pustules the size of a pin-head coloured orange-yellow at first, later black. Protection, or rather prevention, consists of well-balanced nourishment and sufficient potassium.

Black spot

Black spot, or anthracnose, caused by the fungus *Actinonema rosae* (*Marssonia rosae*), is perhaps the most prevalent fungal disease of roses. As early as the beginning of summer brownish-violet spots with typical "blurred" or rayed edges appear on the leaves; later the spots turn black. Attacked leaves turn yellow and fall; sometimes a rose is completely defoliated. Some cultivars are especially prone to this disease, others, such as 'Gloria Dei' or 'Masquerade', appear to be more resistant in European conditions.

Though many firms as well as researchers have tried to find a suitable agent for treating this disease, to date none has proved 100% effective. Growers must therefore rely primarily on prevention, choice of a suitable variety, immediate removal and burning of affected plants, improvement of their nourishment (so the foliage manages to renew itself), and the like.

It is important to keep the roses' environment clean - to refrain from mulching and to rake out all fallen and weeded-out plant refuse.

Diseases of the buds and flowers

In addition to rose mildew, buds and flowers are attacked by grey mould (*Botrytis cinerea*). Sometimes this disease is called bud rot. The flower stalk beneath the bud turns brown and the buds stop growing just before they open, likewise turn brown or also become coated with a greyish layer, and rot. If the bud survives the first invasion, the infection then appears in the form of spots that disfigure the bloom. Plants become infected in an

Black spot

Rosa chinensis
'Viridiflora'

environment that is too damp, especially if the humidity is too high. Attacked parts of the plant must be cut off and burned; a good preventive measure is spraying with fungicides such as Novozir.

Rose growers are averse to most pathological changes but one they definitely favour is *Rosa chinensis* 'Viridiflora', a botanical curiosity amongst roses, which is a feedback documenting the foliar origin of the reproductive organs of higher plants (so-called foliation of the head). *Rosa chinensis* 'Viridiflora' has allegedly been grown in gardens since 1743, other sources state that this mutation did not make its appearance until 1833 in Charleston, South Carolina.

Damage of the growing point sometimes results in deformation of the structure of the inflorescence.

Pests on the roots

Animal pests do not pose such a great danger to roses as fungal diseases. Nevertheless some manage to give growers quite a headache.

The root tissues are sometimes destroyed by the nematode *Meloidogyne marioni*. This can be recognised by the formation of small tumours on the roots and dwarfed growth of the plant. Control consists of disinfecting the soil with nematocides; sometimes also an underplanting of *Tagetes*, which curbs the development of nematodes, helps.

Roots and shoots are often fed on by the weevil *Otiorrhynchus sulcatus*; effective control consists of picking the beetles off the plants.

The neck is often sucked by the aphid *Maculolachnus submacula*, which weakens growth and causes part of the roots to die. Control consists of applying systemic insecticides against aphids.

Pests on the annual shoots and branches

Various scale insects damage the annual shoots and branches of roses by sucking. They form protective scales that are broadly oval to round (*Aulacaspis rosae*) or club-shaped (*Mytilococcus ulmi*) beneath which they hide. Control consists of winter spraying with Arborol-based or other special preparations.

Roses grown in the greenhouse or indoors are subject to attack by whitefly (*Trialeurodes vaporariorum*), pertinacious insects notoriously hard to destroy. These suck the leaves wherever air circulation is poor and the winter temperatures are too high. It is difficult to get rid of these pests because they are resistant to many preparations but they are held in check extremely well by an otherwise ecologically harmless parasitic hymenopterous insect of the genus *Encarsia*.

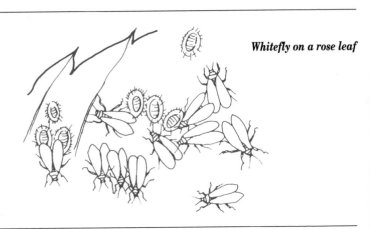

Whitefly on a rose leaf

Gall of Rhodites rosae

The scales of scale insects are generally impervious to water, and contact insecticides do not do much harm. In such cases it is recommended to apply systemic insecticides and simply wait until the insect sucks the preparation from the rose. If there is only a small number of these insects on the annual shoots, remove them in time simply by hand.

On wild roses in natural habitats, on shrub roses, and less often on bedding roses, unusual fringe-like to cotton-like galls coloured green to reddish, brownish with age, and with a peculiar sour musk-like smell sometimes appear. These are the temporary homes of a small hymenopterous insect - the gall-fly *Rhodites rosae* (syn. *Diplolepis rosae*). In spring the female lays eggs in the buds, round which a clump of fibres starts to form. Inside are several chambers in which the larvae slowly develop. The adult gall-flies emerge the following spring. For your peace of mind these galls may be removed, otherwise this gall-fly causes less damage to roses than any of the other hymenopterous pests discussed in the following text.

The stems and annual shoots of roses are also damaged by numerous beetles, mainly weevils such as *Otiorrhynchus singularis*, *Otiorrhynchus sulcatus*, and *Phyllobius oblongus*. These beetles are capable of greatly damaging the surface layers of the stems - literally skinning them.

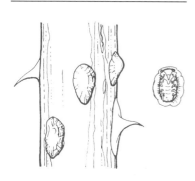

Scale insect on a rose stem

Of the hymenopterous insects it is chiefly sawflies, e.g. *Ardis brunniventris*, that cause the greatest damage to the stems of roses. Its whitish, about 1-cm-long larvae feed on the pith from the top downward so that the attacked parts wilt and dry up. Adult insects lay eggs under the epidermis of the leaves. The best means of control is to remove wilting shoots so the larvae cannot develop into adults.

Rose buds are fed on by the gall-midge *Thomasiniana oculiperda*. It usually attacks newly budded roses where the larvae suck the sap at the point of the bud union. All that is often required to control this pest is covering the bud union with grafting wax.

Pests of rose leaves

If the leaves are dotted with whitish blobs on the upper surface and have small pale-green insects on the underside, usually it is the leaf hopper *Typhlocyba rosae*. As a rule, this pest can be controlled with the usual insecticides for homopterous insects.

Close by the leaves typically curled lengthwise along the midrib is the larva of Blennocampa pusilla and a section of the pupa.

Rose sawfly and feeding damage of its caterpillars on the rose leaves.

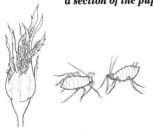

Aphids prey chiefly on buds that are still green

Adult, larva, and eggs of a gall-midge

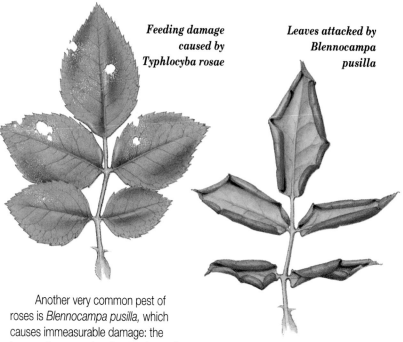

Feeding damage caused by Typhlocyba rosae

Leaves attacked by Blennocampa pusilla

Another very common pest of roses is *Blennocampa pusilla,* which causes immeasurable damage: the leaves of roses curl up lengthwise until in the end they form a tube. Affected leaves should be removed immediately and at the first signs of the pest the rose bushes should be sprayed with an insecticide.

Sometimes the leaves are irregularly deformed, riddled with holes and blisters. This is caused by a leaf bug of the genus *Lygus*: it, too, should be sprayed with an insecticide as soon as signs of it appear on the bush.

Pests of the buds and flowers

Probably the most prevalent pest of flowers as well as flower stalks is the aphid *Macrosiphium rosae*. Sometimes flower stalks are veritably coated with them. They measure about 4 mm and are coloured reddish or green. Currently a good means of control is spraying with Pirimor and similar preparations.

Buds are often attacked by the strawberry blossom weevil (*Anthonomus rubi*). The females first of all bite the flower stalk and then lay their eggs inside the bud. Generally the bud soon falls and the larva devours its contents. Control consists of timely collecting and destroying the affected buds; spraying with chemical preparations is usually not effective.

Flowers are also damaged by various thrips, such as *Thrips physapus*. These suck the sap in the flowers and cause white spots on the petals or premature drying of the buds. It is necessary to look for special insecticides.

Roses in garden design

Though cultivated varieties have been grown in gardens for merely two centuries, roses are a classic component in garden design, one that imparts to the garden a nostalgic or Old World element. I cannot explain it but whenever I see roses in a garden, even one designed along ultra-modern lines, I feel as if it is those roses that represent a certain continuity, a connecting link between the old and the new. Quite possibly it is a sort of subconscious reminiscence having to do with the fairy tale Sleeping Beauty, perhaps only because I have been working with roses more than half my lifetime, or perhaps because in my mind's eye I envision the rose garden of Empress Josephine at Malmaison (though I have never been there) and envy her the dozens, nay hundreds of old cultivars of the Gallic rose (*Rosa gallica*) and moss rose (*Rosa* x *centifolia*) that she gathered together there long before the advent of modern roses. That, so it seems, was an irrepeatable attempt to bring together the whole of the then existing assortment of European cultivated roses.

Roses are nowadays grown by thousands, perhaps tens of thousands of people. For about eleven years I was a corresponding member of the American Rose Society (ARS). These associations and societies and their members are usually concerned with collecting and growing individual cultivars, collecting bordering on competition as to who has the greatest number of cultivars. Only very occasionally did I read in the ARS yearbooks anything about the many uses of roses in garden design.

However, one must add that there is a certain discouraging aspect: incorporating roses in garden design is not at all easy and sometimes even quite a difficult task as many rose gardens, past and present, testify. Their texture, structure, shape, colours, and scents make roses such singular flowers that they do not tolerate the competition of others very well. Not that they would not pass the test but rather they would be overshadowed. And so I must confess that the loveliest rose garden I have ever seen (and take that as my personal opinion) is the one in the Moravian city of Olomouc. There the roses are monothematically planted in large neutral blocks of structural concrete that do not appear massive but purely as functional elements, and the only "competing" element are the expanses of water. Only here was I conscious of the immense innate character of the rose.

Architectural use

How, then, can roses best be used in garden design? Note that I do not speak of gardens but of garden design. In a garden, be it ornamental or intended for just rest and relaxation, everybody can plant what he wants, what reflects his tastes, his image, his personality, his likes.

A cultivated climbing rose is just as suitable for a chateau arch (rose garden in Baden-Baden) as for a rustic gateway.

In well-thought-out garden design, roses should always be used in large expanses of uniform composition consisting of specimens of the same shape and colour. Bedding roses planted in a single large bed of at least 10 m², but preferably larger, have the effect of a bombshell. A bed in which there are only one or two specimens of various different cultivars creates a neurotic, chaotic, restless effect, even though it may seem beautiful to those who like bright and cheerful colours. However: What is beauty?

For climbing roses, garden design has a "third dimension". Whereas bedding roses can truly be used only in flat, two-dimensional compositions, climbing roses can be trained up a suitable support all the way to the top of a house and for at least half the year they can be an interesting component

'Grand' mère Jenny' (Meilland 1960) - hybrid tea. As the offspring of 'Gloria Dei' it has pink-edged petals.

Classic rose gardens (for example in Charlottenburg) incorporated all the various types of roses - from bedding roses to standard roses.

'Weisse Innensee' is used as a so-called carpeting rose that trails over the ground with branches rising to a height of barely 30 cm.

of the facade and architecture of the building. Roses on various free-standing supporting constructions should always have some function: shading an arbour or archway, bordering a pathway, as a solitary ornamental element on a lawn. In the case of climbing roses I am surprisingly not as insistent on a single block of colour and am willing to tolerate a different cultivar on each supporting structure. Do you know the reason why?

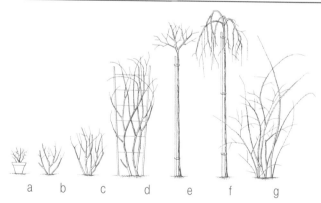

Basic shapes of cultivated roses that should be taken into account in garden design: a - miniature rose, b - Polyantha, c - hybrid tea, d - climbing rose, e - standard rose, f - umbrella rose (or weeping tree rose), g - shrub rose.

Climbing roses soften even the lines of relatively severe architecture.

Immersing cut roses wrapped in newspaper in a little cold water at the bottom of the bathtub

Well, it is because climbing roses produce perhaps hundreds of blooms on their long main stems, illustrating my claim that large numbers of flowers, providing repetition of shape and colour, will make any rose stand out.

A true exception to the rule are the so-called shrub or species roses: these can stand as solitary specimens - a dominant feature in an expanse of lawn, or, especially white-flowered or yellow-flowered specimens, against a background of dark conifers.

Roses are an excellent material for blocking access to certain areas. The thorns of roses planted thus do their work well - no one will take a shortcut through there. However, this also has its drawback: who will care for such shrubs, trim them, remove windblown bits of paper and other rubbish, etc.?

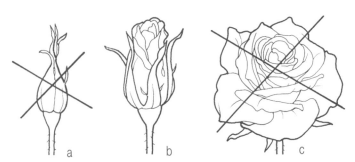

The right time to cut roses: a - too early, b - right time, c - too late.

A single rose with an added touch of greenery

A special role is played by roses in another domain of modern society: as greenery alongside motorways. One species that is found planted alongside motorways as well as on the central reservation probably throughout all of Europe is the Japanese apple rose (*Rosa rugosa*) native to the Far East. At the same time it is not one of those plants drivers would want to stop for and pick to take home (thereby endangering traffic) and the main stems are so pliable that if a car crashes into them in an accident they'll bend aside, cushion the impact, and a person comes out of it all with, say, only a few thorns under his skin...

Roses in the home

Where else but in the chapter on design should one include a few lines about roses in the home. First and foremost it is the rose as a cut flower in a vase. Once again I call attention to the distinctiveness of the rose and recommend you choose a suitable vase, one that will complement it. A rose does not deserve to be a supplement to an ornamental vase, it itself should rather be the dominating element - or it should at least form such a harmonious whole with the vase that the one would be unthinkable without the other.

Not every rose is good for cutting or suits every vase. A tall vase requires a long-stemmed rose terminated by a single bloom. Into round vases one can put a large bouquet of multiflowered bedding roses. The best time to gather blooms, according to current experience, is not in the cool of the morning but in the evening. The stems must be put in water immediately and kept in a cool place until they are to be put in a vase. Large firms keep them in coolers at a temperature of about 5 °C, at home I have found that a good method is to wrap the cut roses in newspapers and lay them in about 4-5 cm of cool water in the bathtub overnight. Remove all the leaves of purchased or cut roses that would be below water level and cut off the bottom of the stem with a long sloping cut (about 3 cm long).

How long flowers will last in the vase depends not only on the maturity of the blooms but also on the cultivar.

Of late it has been possible to make the flowers last longer by adding a suitable life-prolonging preparation (the brand name differs in each country) to the water. Sometimes all that is needed is to add a small amount of sugar (15 g/litre). Unless a suitable preparation has been added, the water in the vase should be changed daily, the vase should not stand in a cold room, and it should not be exposed to direct sunlight. Should one so wish, the roses

can always be taken out of the vase for the night, wrapped in newspapers and immersed in water in the bathtub, or else wrapped in wet newspapers and laid in the cellar.

A bouquet of roses is best if it is a single colour. It is even said that individual rose cultivars do not tolerate one another.

View this closing chapter not as one of instruction and information - that purpose was served by what went before. What I wanted was to indicate here that you must find your own way to the rose, just like to your intended, and almost always the way is full of thorns. And I also wanted to show that faithfulness to a single colour (or hue) will perhaps bring you more enjoyment than colour promiscuity.

Take your pick - and whichever rose you choose, tend it with care.

Like Saint-Exupéry's Little Prince.

Biedermeier-style
wedding bouquet

Index

Index